STONEHENGE

A guide to the world's greatest megalithic site

Damien Pryor

History, cultural significance, alignments
and shadow-fields.

Also available by this author:
The Great Pyramid and the Sphinx
The Externsteine: Europe's greatest Celtic site
Lalibela in thirteenth century Ethiopia
The tropical zodiac, its origin and validity

© 2011 Threshold Publishing

ISBN ISBN 9780958134187

CONTENTS

Later Stonehenge (stages III +) & its shadow-fields
Stonehenge as a shadow-field observatory

Conclusion: the many purposes of Stonehenge

Appendix
The Saros cycle and atmospheric Carbon 14

References

Illustration credits

Index

Chapter One: The background to Stonehenge

The Megalithic people and the Celts

Stonehenge is the best-known Megalithic site in the world. But the purpose behind its unique stone circles is not well understood. Stonehenge is situated about 85 miles (137 km) southwest of London, on the Wiltshire Plains in southern England. Its circles of stones, created with huge effort thousands of years ago, have been an intriguing enigma to tourists for centuries. Recent archaeological theories only focus on the limited use of Stonehenge as a burial site. And indeed the after-life was part of its purpose, but as we shall see later, burial and after-death rites were not the main purpose of this great site. In the 1960's it was shown by the academic astronomer Dr. Hawkins, that Stonehenge was some kind of astronomical observatory. It was because of this closeness of the site to the realms of gods, that people sought to have a burial site in its vicinity.

Most people feel that this discovery of Hawkins is exciting and tremendously important. However it is hard to find a book where unfounded theories are separated from fact, and the actual astronomical events to which Stonehenge is oriented clearly shown. And it is even harder to find a book where the reasons are given as to why such celestial cycles actually interested the Megalithic builders of millennia ago.

Once we know what these observation capacities really are, the question arises, just why did these people want to make such observations! The more we know about its extraordinary alignments, the more questions we have. Why did the Megalithic stone circle builders in ancient Britain, and elsewhere, monitor celestial cycles with such intense interest? Why did people from the pre-Grecian Mystery centres such as Mycenae visit Stonehenge, about 3,500 years ago?

In this book we shall find out the answers to these questions. Specially designed graphics show in a living way the focus of the alignments of Stonehenge. And the multi-purpose nature of Stonehenge becomes clear, too. And we will discover a new secret of Stonehenge, its shadow-fields. We can then really appreciate not only its amazing construction, but also find an answer as to why, starting some 5,000 years ago on the wind-swept plains of Salisbury, the ancient ancestors of the British people went to such effort to construct stone circles. But first we will get some background information, by looking at some sacred sites that have similar qualities to Stonehenge. Such sites are megalithic in character, that is they are constructed from stones, usually roughly hewn and often of considerable size, with little or no artistic embellishment.

These are found especially in Britain and at Carnac in France. They are designed to facilitate awareness of celestial influences at work in nature, during the cycle of the year. It is evident from the design of these sites that the people who built them saw a spiritual side to nature. So the cycle of the seasons required that the priests undertook interaction with some kind of spiritual influences from the moon, the sun, the planets or the stars.

The Megalithic people in the UK and on the coast of Western Europe about 3,000 BC began constructing their stone monuments. In building their sacred sites, these people had several purposes in mind. One purpose for which they constructed their monuments concerned the plight of the soul in life after death. Monuments built at such sites are therefore rightly called tombs, and were often constructed as underground chambers, sometimes of considerable size. There are many of these tombs on the Salisbury Plains around Stonehenge. They often had an orientation towards a star or the rising sun.

But a second type of monument, of rough stone chambers, was also constructed; and these had a different purpose. These monuments don't appear to have served as tombs. These were intended to facilitate the process of spiritual interaction with cosmic influences. These chambers were either above or below the ground, and they may have an astronomical orientation. A third type of monument is the stone circle, which is concerned with interaction of cosmic forces with the Earth's own subtle energies, in their ebb and flow during the seasonal cycle.

To gain a clearer understanding of the motivation for the Megalithic priests wanting to monitor such processes, we need to enter into the way of experiencing the seasonal cycle of priests of ancient times. Later we shall explore the actual astronomical observations possible from Stonehenge, the stone alignments that identified the solstices, the equinoxes and the time of an eclipse, etc. But, as we shall see, it is also a fact that the sunlight would cast large shadows, precisely because of the use of huge stones at Stonehenge (and elsewhere).

A new and important question will be explored here. Were they looking into the shadows, as well as the light? Through the positions of their stones, did they also create large shadow-fields, which blocked out the light, not only alignments to key celestial processes? This question will allow us to find out what is really so interesting about Stonehenge and other similar sites.

But first of all, let's get clear about terminology. Old British sites are often referred to as "Celtic" as if these were a group of people unique to the British Isles. But the Celts were found throughout a large part of Europe, not only Britain. In the course of many centuries, these people often intermarried with indigenous people. However, it has been a British custom to designate as "Celtic" only that small portion of this large ethnic group which migrated into Britain from the Continent some 2,000 years ago. But this custom is basically incorrect, as the term "Celtic" refers to a very large group of people, who existed for millennia on the Continent.

In Britain starting about 3,000 years BC, sacred sites such as Stonehenge were built by the Megalithic people who were indigenous to Britain. The civilisation responsible for building

Stonehenge and most of the other features of this area, are known as the Wessex people. The religion of the Wessex people is not unlike that of the old indigenous Europeans, the ancient Celts. But, since Stonehenge was built some 2,000 years prior to the time of the so-called Celts of Britain, it is more correct to define the builders of Stonehenge as the Megalithic people. This term simply means people who built sacred sites using large slabs of rock.

The priests of the Megalithic people who were in charge of Stonehenge are often referred to as Druids. But scholars have pointed out that the earliest historical references to the Druids are found only as far back as the time of the Roman Empire. However it is quite possible that the Druids existed long before then, without any historical references being made to them, for historical records about Britain are scarce before the Roman wars in Britain. So, we shall refer to the priests of the Wessex people as Druids.

Stonehenge was constructed by the Megalithic people, who no doubt had a view of life and nature similar to that of the later Celtic people of Britain, descendants of the widespread Continental Celts. The Megalithic people had a living religious feeling for the seasonal cycle and various celestial influences and associated spirit beings. Their sites are found mainly in Britain and France, especially at Stonehenge, Callanish, Maes Howe and Carnac.

The spirituality of the Megalithic people
Most of the artworks for the period are very elementary, but a few artworks have been discovered in Europe that give us a general indication of the spirituality of the ancient people living three to six thousand years ago, during the Neolithic Age and into the Bronze Age. It was amongst these people, on the western seaboard of Europe, that Megalithic sites were constructed. A very striking artefact from these times is the ancient Nebra disc found in Germany; a bronze disc about 30 cm in diameter, dating from approx. 1,600 BC. It depicts some stars, including the Pleiades, as well as the moon, the sun and

a sun boat (like the solar bark of the ancient Egyptians). But it also depicts the position of the solstice sunrise points, showing the intense focus of the religion on the cosmic influences operative between the Earth and the cosmos.

And there is an ancient stone circle site in Goseck, Germany, constructed about 5,000 BC. It consists of four concentric circles, a mound and two wooden palisades, and served a similar function to Stonehenge. It was designed to facilitate interaction with cosmic influences affecting the Earth during the seasonal cycle. It is obvious that Stonehenge was also used for similar purposes, and this includes rituals for the after-life too. Ancient British artefacts from the same general period with artistic features are very few. But the stone ball of Towie in Aberdeenshire, which shows a series of well-designed and executed concentric spirals and swirls testifies to a belief in some sort of swirling life-energies.

But later Celtic artworks from Britain or the Continent, which date from about 1,400 BC to about 100AD, also indirectly give us an indication of the spirituality of the earlier Megalithic people. These artworks depict various spirit beings and the interaction of an initiate-priest or shaman with these beings. A striking example is the ancient copper bowl found in Denmark called the Gundestrup Cauldron, which shows a series of initiatory scenes where a priest interacts with various spirit beings. Many other Celtic artworks exist depicting similar spirit beings, on such items as ceremonial belt buckles bronze mirrors and pottery.

In Britain the nature-mysticism of the Megalithic people echoed on amongst those groups who became known as the British Celts, and literature about their mystical spiritual beliefs and practises has survived. As a result, fascinating glimpses of the mystical beliefs of the Megalithic people can be found in old Welsh texts, such as the Mabinogion or in poetry about the famous Cumbrian seer, Taliesin.

These old texts, dating back to about the 6th century, would echo to some extent the mystical views of the much earlier Megalithic people, the people who built the stone circles and underground chambers. In various old Welsh mystical poems there are allusions to spirit beings and spiritual processes. In this 6th century literature there are many references to spiritual beings, including nature spirits, to mystical experiences and initiatory processes. (1) The nature spirits eventually became famous in 19th century children's literature as the inhabitants of the realm of Faery.

The collection known as the Myvyrian Archaiology is especially rich in mystical themes. For example, in an account concerning the spiritual adventures of one Tuan Mac Cairell, there are allusions to spirit beings and also to an initiatory three-day sleep. During these days, it was believed that his soul is set free of his body, and he enters the Otherworld, also called the Netherworld, the realm where the souls of the dead dwell. Tuan is a shaman-like character, and he tells how on one occasion he undergoes a sleep for three-days and three nights and in this process, he became (or believed he became) a fish living in the river:

> "Then I fasted for three-days and three nights, when sleep fell upon me. And I passed into the shape of a river salmon, there and then." (2)

In this mystical literature, there is also a realm called Annwyn or Annwfn, a realm so far in the West that almost no one could reach it; only by dying was it reachable. So it was the Netherworld, the realm of the Dead, and hence it was also the realm which the initiated reached. For in Hellenistic cultures the realm of the dead was exactly the realm that the Greeks heroes alone could enter. Heroes such as Hercules and Odysseus descended into the Netherworld as part of their initiatory experiences.

In a 7th century Welsh poem, Gododdin, written by Nennius there is the tale of how King Arthur descended into this

Underworld with some of his knights. (3) In another one of these poems, "The spoils of Annwyn" ascribed to Taliesin, translated by Skene in the Four Ancient Books of Wales, various esoteric experiences occur, which infer the transference of consciousness beyond the world accessible to our senses and into some spiritual realm, including the Netherworld. (4) So when we consider Stonehenge and other Megalithic sites, the strong probability exists that these were constructed for spiritual initiatory purposes and for rituals to do with the after-life.

Monuments designed for religious purposes
In Britain and Brittany it appears that some rough stone chambers were made specifically for a spiritual purpose, and not to serve as graves. In such places the acolyte would undergo a secret process, probably three days in duration, similar to the experience hinted at in the above quote from the Myvyrian Archaiology. With this kind of megalithic monument, the type used for a spiritual purpose, we enter the same kind of problem as with Stonehenge (and with the Great Pyramid). Is the monument only used a part of rituals to do with the cult of the dead, or is it designed for an initiatory purpose also?

There is a sacred site in the remote Orkney Islands, north of Scotland, which can be used to illustrate this problem. This is the so-called Dwarfie Stane (dwarf stone) at the base of Ward Hill, located on the island of Hoy. It is a large and striking rock monument, and is usually classified as a tomb. It's an oblong block of sandstone measuring 28 feet (8.5m) long, 13 feet (4m) wide and 6.5 feet (2m) high. It has a square doorway and inside, it has been hollowed out to form a short tunnel leading to two separate chambers. For some really useful information and pictures of this site, see Sigurd Towrie's site: http://www.orkneyjar.com/

Outside, there is a sandstone block that is designed to seal the doorway, and it is an unusual monument as Sigurd Towrie points out:

> What makes the Dwarfie Stane remarkable is the fact that the massive stone was hollowed out using nothing but stone or deer antler tools, muscle power and patience. An opening, three feet square, is cut into the middle of the stone's west face and leads into the inner chamber. This chamber contains two rock-cut spaces resembling bed-places, both of which are too short for anyone of a normal stature. These were undoubtedly responsible for the origin of the dwarf folklore that surrounds the site. (www.orkneyjar.com/orkney)

And there is also an acoustic quality here, as the Aaron Watson Archaeology Research webpage mentions:

> The Dwarfie Stane in Orkney has a short passage and chamber that was tunnelled into a solid block of stone. It is the only example of its kind known in the British Isles. The solid walls and confined chamber constitute a very resonant space, and it is possible to create intense effects using the voice alone. While standing waves were dramatic inside, some effects were not confined to the chamber. With some sound frequencies, listeners on the roof perceived the stone itself to be shaking. This is most likely an illusion, with the sounds resonating the listeners themselves.

The potential for sounds to create this kind of experience raises some interesting questions as to how such experiences were understood in the Neolithic. Loud sounds generated outside the Dwarfie Stane, such as beating a drum, generated powerful echoes that echoed like thunder around the surrounding cliffs and hillsides. While the choice of this location would have been determined by the availability of a sufficiently large stone, the spectacular setting and impressive echoes contribute to the experience of this unique monument. (5)

8

http://www.monumental.uk.com/site/research/proj/acoustics/dwarfie.html

It is clear that this hollowed-out stone could have been a burial site, but it is actually far more suited to some kind of ritual connected with an initiatory procedure. However this theme is not usually focussed on in mainstream archaeology, so it is classified as a tomb. Yet Megalithic people were focused both on the after-death process and on subtle seasonal energies in their sacred sites. In the Orkney Islands, there is another example of a sacred site that has a chamber for initiatory experience, as well as upright stones for observation of subtle seasonal energies. It is the Megalithic complex at Maes Howe.

Sacred site on the Orkneys
The Maes Howe site was similar in some way to Stonehenge, in that it was designed to provide celestial observations. So it has a line-of-sight to the distant midwinter setting sun (the Yuletide sun). But it also offers a protective chamber that may have been intended for the three-day sleep process. This place is on the island of Hoy, in the Orkney Islands, and comprises the tomb of Maes Howe, the sacred circle of Stenness, and a large upright stone, the Barnhouse Stone. The tomb is a substantial rock-lined mound with a passageway that is oriented towards the setting sun at the winter solstices. A good site for pictures and data about Maeshow is http://www.orkneyjar.com/history/maeshowe/index.html.

The Maeshowe monument was conical in shape, with a deep depression in the top; it had a diameter of about 100 ft (30m) and stood 36 feet or 11 metres high. This monument is now regarded as a tomb, yet no remains of bodies have ever been found there and, more significantly, the design of the site called for the entrance to be blocked by a stone, which is still there. But this is a stone which leaves enough space to allow access by people. The space is some 3 feet wide (.9m) and 1½ ft high (.5m).

This indicates that the monument was designed for religious ritualistic purpose rather than a tomb. For such a gap is inappropriate in a tomb designed to protect a deceased person, but it is sufficient to allow a person to enter and to position themselves in the chamber to witness the last rays of the setting sun on the winter solstice. For the midwinter sun can shine deeply into this chamber…

> "In the weeks leading up to the winter solstice, the darkest time of the Orcadian year, the last rays of the setting sun shine through the entrance passage to pierce the darkness of the chambered cairn. It has now been shown that the centre axis of the inner entrance passage is directly aligned with the centre of the Barnhouse Stone. From here, the line travels out to strike Ward Hill on Hoy at a place where the sun set 22 days before and after the winter solstice. Recent research at Maeshowe revealed another interesting solar phenomenon - a period when the setting sun briefly reappears from the side of Hoy's Ward Hill before disappearing beneath the horizon. This phenomenon has been christened "flashing", from the flashes of light apparently seen within the cairn." (6)
> http://www.orkneyjar.com/history/maeshowe/index.html

That this chamber was not a gravesite but an initiatory site appears the more likely situation, especially as it is integrated into a larger complex of spiritual sites:

> At the nearby standing Stones of Stenness, are two angular slabs, standing side by side, with a large prone stone beside them. It is intriguing, although perhaps mere coincidence, that when viewed from the centre of the stone circle, Maeshowe is aligned to the gap between the two "dolmen stones". (7)

So, at Maes Howe and at the Dwarfie Stane, there are two monuments designed as initiatory sites, not burial places. Furthermore, at Maes Howe, the stone henge with a diameter of 32 yards (29m), has an outer circle with originally 12 standing stones. On the basis of what we have suggested above, as the general outlook on the cosmos of the Megalithic people, this site in the Orkneys appears to have been a major sacred site, and is a smaller proto-type of Stonehenge. This henge has ditch around it, about 6ft (1.8m) deep, which all the megalithic sacred sites have. But the question arises, whether the various old Megalithic stone circles were arranged in a circle as a reflection not only of the spherical shape of the night sky, but possibly also of the zodiac?

Chapter Two: Sites for observing celestial cycles

British Stone Circles or Henges

What is a henge? A henge is an archaeological term to mean "any banked, ditched, enclosure". Many henges were built in Britain, and many of these later had a circle of upright stones placed in them. Circular rings have been made from standing stones in many places in northern Britain, and of course at Stonehenge is the most famous of such circular menhir sites. As we can learn from an excellent website (Archtext) on British monuments, many large henges were constructed by the Megalithic people:

> In Scotland the Ring of Brodgar is one of the most striking henges. It is on the Mainland Island in Orkney and consists of a ditch with no bank broken by two entrances and is about 122 yards (112m) in diameter. Inside was later placed a ring, originally, of some sixty upright stones with an average height of two metres. In Ireland there is a henge in Co. Down at Ballynahatty called Giant's Ring. The diameter is 200 yards (183m) and the bank built of material scraped up from the interior is ca. 22 yards (20m) wide at the base and ca. 3.8 yards (3.5m) in height.

Some of these henges were much bigger than Stonehenge:

> At Knowlton on the Salisbury plains, in an area that was apparently sacred at the time, three henges arranged in the characteristic almost straight line are surrounded by groups of later round barrows. The southern circle has a diameter of ca. 262 yards (240m) with a ditch on the inside and two entrances. To the north the central circle has a diameter of around 115 yards (105m) with two entrances with a bank today about four metres high and the ditch about 10.5 metres wide. In the middle of the enclosure are the ruins of a medieval church measuring about 90 yards (82m).

Another site, even more extensive, had a circle made of wooden posts, not stones:

> Mount Pleasant henge is one of the large Wessex henges and lies about a mile east of Dorchester. Its bank was originally about 13ft (4m) surrounding an egg-shaped enclosure about 405 yards (370m) along its longer axis and about 350 yards (320m) along the shorter one. Originally the area, comprising 4.8 hectares, was entered by four entrances. Outside the bank is a ditch that has a diameter of about 47 yards (43m).
>
> Within the enclosure were the remains of a circular timber structure consisting of five concentric rings of postholes which date from round about 2000 BC. Within and running parallel to the main ditch about twelve metres away a palisade foundation ditch was dug. The palisade itself must have been a major engineering job as some 1,600 oaken posts would have been required.

It is clear that the Megalithic people constructed many sacred sites, some of which were much larger than Stonehenge. Another henge at Hindwell, near New Radnor in Powys was an egg-shaped oval with a perimeter of over a mile in length (2.5km), with a diameter of some 875 yards (800m) and covered an area of 34 hectares. At its western end was the entrance flanked by enormous timber posts facing towards the sunset on Midsummer Day. For more about such henges see the Archtext website (8),
http://www.archtext.co.uk/onlinetexts/britains_past/chapter07

Megalithic sites and the stars
Since various of these old sites throughout Britain have twelve standing stones, some people have concluded that this indicates a zodiacal interest, but there is of course no literary evidence from the pre-literate Megalithic peoples to back this

up. And yet it appears that the number of sites with twelve stones is more than just coincidence.

There may have originally been more sites with twelve stones, but this cannot now be known, as so many of these sites are in a state of disrepair. But at Stenness it appears to be the case that there were 12 stones, even if archaeological research is correct in concluding that one of the twelve stones was never actually erected.

At Avebury, the largest of the British stone circle sites, the innermost circle consisted of 12 stones, and the inner circle had 27 stones, which may be connected to the lunar cycle. Then there is the huge site at Stanton Drew in Somerset, which apparently once had nine concentric circles of upright stones.

One of the main three circles at this site, some 43 metres wide, had 12 stones; most of the other circles were marked out with far less emphasis. Another stone circle is at a lesser known, remote but significant Megalithic complex. It is near the village of Drizzlecombe in Dartmoor, where there are two stone circles, 30 metres in diameter. One circle has 12 standing stones, the other has 13 stones, and there are also single standing stones and rock cairns.

In Scotland a 12-stone circle is located at Croft Moraig, and another was constructed at Rhinns of Islay, although for a long time the stones have been recumbent. In Ireland in County Sligo, at the large Carrowmore Complex, which has over 100 monuments, including tombs and cairns, there is a circle which once had 12 standing stones. And at Reanascreena in County Cork is another intact 12-stone site.

If more of these ancient sites had remained intact, it is certain that many of them would have shown the use of twelve standing stones. Another prominent number is 30, which may relate to the 30-year cycle of Saturn's orbiting around our skies, viewed geocentrically.

It is curious in regard to the 12 stones of Henness in the Orkneys, that in old mystical literature, Sir Gawain the famous Arthurian-Grail hero is said to have lived in the Orkneys. His father was the king of the Orkney Islands. There are of course, twelve main Arthurian knights, each of whom had a seat at the famous Round Table. Many commentators see this as a reference to the zodiac. But as we have no written records from the Megalithic people on any subject, the zodiac connection has to remain a theory.

Megalithic sites for the souls of the dead
As with all other earlier peoples, the Megalithic people placed great importance on the journey in the after-life. But with their old holistic consciousness, they also placed great significance on the influence of the stars or planets, both for the living and for the dead. Many of their tombs are aligned to a significant star, or sunrise or sunset. This is a fact that was observed and researched already in the late 19th century. Various scientists and other interested researchers ascertained that the Megalithic people always oriented their tombs towards the solstitial or equinoctial sunsets or sunrises, or the extreme moon positions of rising and setting known as standstills, or to the point where a prominent star rose or set.

A striking example of such a cairn made by the Megalithic people is to be found in Kintraw on the west coast of Scotland. This tomb actually has a false entrance (or rather, a false exit) on its south-west side. At this tomb two tall upright stones stand at the side of a flat broad door (a slab of stone) which goes nowhere, for behind it there is simply solid rock and earth. But a deceased soul, in the centre of the tomb, looking out through this doorway, would be aligned to the moonset in the south-west, at a key point in its orbital path! (The point is known as a Standstill, see a later section.) So, it is in effect, a cosmic alignment designed for the use of a spirit being, namely a disembodied soul! (9) But nearby is a 12 ft (3.7m) standing stone with an approximate alignment to the summer sunrise.

It is possible that this stone was not intended for the deceased, but for living people to use in spiritual observation of nature (the summer sunrise, etc). This is precisely the enigma of the Megalithic people and their sacred sites: are they only to do with the dead, or are they also intended for religious purposes including celestial observation? At the present time, the main archaeological theories about Stonehenge argue that it was constructed primarily for the dead.

But we shall see, this view is incorrect because it fails to account for the complex celestial alignments associated with lunar and solar cycles and with seasonal changes. All of these alignments required a huge effort to create, and together with the shadow-fields, are the main purpose of Stonehenge. A good site about Kintraw and all Megalithic sites in general is http://www.megalithic.co.uk/

At some time in its history Stonehenge was used for burials. Some sixty cremated remains were buried along the ditch, but there were certainly further burial sites here. Archaeologists from Sheffield University state that, "Stonehenge was the largest cemetery in Britain at the time, containing ashes from about 250 cremations." (15) So Stonehenge was a sacred site also in the sense of a burial ground; however 250 is a very small number for a monument that was in use for about 2,000 years.

This indicates again that the primary purpose of Stonehenge was for monitoring of celestial cycles and associated rites. Stonehenge was certainly integrated into a much larger sacred area, with other temples and many burial sites on the Wiltshire plains. This is the case with other great sacred sites that were established for religious rites and festivals connected to the seasonal cycle and the movements of the sun, moon and stars. Since the souls of the dead journey into these same realms where the moon, sun and stars are found, people felt that it was comforting for their grave to be near to this site.

Stonehenge: part of a large sacred site

Why is Stonehenge special, and why is it called Stonehenge? Well somewhat confusingly, the term henge as used in the word "Stonehenge", comes from old Saxon and apparently it means hanging or suspended. So *Stonehenge* may possibly mean hanging stones; because at Stonehenge some of the stones, namely the horizontal ones that cap the uprights, are held up above the ground. And this arrangement is unique in all of Britain. No other henge with a circle of menhirs or upright stones was ever given such capstones. However the word henge today usually means a roughly circular area that has been enclosed deliberately by an earthwork, a kind of embankment which also has a resulting ditch; and Stonehenge also has this too.

With its double concentric stone-ring appearance, Stonehenge is well known across the globe. The monument has been rather poorly protected in earlier centuries. In the 19th century, one could even rent a hammer to smash off a piece from the stones. (!) And a road was constructed very close to the Heel Stone, and an underground telephone line was installed perilously close to the site. As well, the tourist car park is built right on top of another, very ancient sacred site. But in recent years much effort has been made to improve this situation. Today the monument is protected by English Heritage, and access to the stones themselves is restricted.

But why is Stonehenge so famous? What is special about it? As we have noted above, there were many such sites, and some were much larger. There are several factors that make Stonehenge very special. Some of these are obvious whilst others are not so easy to see. It is obvious that Stonehenge is the only stone circle in which an exceptional amount of effort has gone into carving the uprights into shaped slabs, not leaving them as irregular natural stones. Secondly it is the only site where lintel stones have been placed onto the upright stones to cap them, and these have been carved so that they have a circular profile, giving the circle a more rounded appearance.

Thirdly, the capstones, and their upright recipients have been actually carved in the manner of wood carpentry, in order to ensure a safe and accurate placing of the horizontal slabs up on top of the menhirs. Fourthly, the stones are of two distinct types. One type is the bluestone that is not from the local area at all, but come from 140 miles away; this means that a truly huge effort was made to get them to Wiltshire. The other special qualities of Stonehenge are its exceptional astronomical monitoring capacity.

This will become clear as we explore its astronomical features. Most people will have heard that Stonehenge is an astronomical observatory, but this idea is often only vaguely understood. In this book, we shall show very clearly the celestial alignments of Stonehenge, and then find out why they went to such trouble to create these. A good way to discover the extraordinary features of Stonehenge is to ask, what really caused the Megalithic people to build Stonehenge on the site where it is? To answer this question, we need to get some clarity about the environment where it was built, and secondly we need to know the structural phases that Stonehenge went through over the centuries. This will lead us to discover what the Megalithic people wanted to do at Stonehenge.

The first point to note about Stonehenge is that its site on the Salisbury plains was not an isolated sacred site; it was not built on bare, empty plains. Several extraordinary sacred sites were also situated in the area around Stonehenge, or were built during its early stage of development. In this area some 400 tombs are located, both the round barrow type and the long barrow type. But in fact, we can go much further back in time, to about 8,000 BC. As John Wood points out,

> Archaeologists have found four (or possibly five, although one may have been a natural tree throw) large Mesolithic postholes that date to around 8000 BC nearby, beneath the modern tourist car park. These held pine posts around 0.75 metres (2.5 ft) in diameter that were erected and left to rot in situ. Three of the

posts (and possibly four) were in an east-west alignment and may have had ritual significance; no parallels are known from Britain at the time but similar sites have been found in Scandinavia. (10)
http://www.themystica.com/mystica/

Durrington Walls, Woodhenge
Returning now to the time of early Stonehenge, there were other sacred sites constructed in this area in addition to the numerous tombs or burial sites. And recent archaeological research in the area has started to uncover more remarkable sites near Stonehenge. Only 1.8 miles (3kms) from Stonehenge the remains of a town have been discovered, at Durrington Walls, which was built about 2,600-2,500 BC. This village also had its sacred henge; a nearly oval shaped 12-hectare enclosure surrounded by a ditch with an external bank about 32 yards (30m) wide and about 10 ft (3 m) high. But in addition to this site, alongside the henge, there were also two large wooden circular buildings, of a ceremonial kind. One of these had a diameter of 32 yards, and probably had a cone-shaped sloping roof.

It has been calculated that to build this, some 10 acres (4 hectares) of woodlands had to be felled. (11) In the valley nearby was a village of about a thousand dwellings. This means that it was one of the largest towns in the Stone Age. Archaeologists conclude that it was here that the people who built Stonehenge lived, and also that many people came to stay at Durrington for important festivals which were held at Stonehenge, (and at the Durrington temple, as long as this wooden temple lasted).

Many artefacts and remains of meal times can be found at Durrington; whereas at Stonehenge itself, because only solemn sacred activities took place, no archaeological evidence of everyday living can be found. Durrington's timber circle was aligned with the winter solstice sunrise, the opposite of Stonehenge, which is oriented to the summer sunrise. However it is quite incorrect to define Stonehenge as a summer solstice site and to then see it as a contrast to Durrington, being a winter solstice site because as we shall discover, Stonehenge was aligned to much more than the summer solstice.

There was yet another feature to this Durrington, a feature which is also found at Stonehenge, namely a large processional way, or avenue linking the round temple building to the Avon river. See illustration 1 for a clear view of the various sacred sites that were located near Stonehenge. The processional way of Durrington, like that of Stonehenge, could have been used for burial ceremonies as well as other spiritual rites. As a prominent Stonehenge archaeologist, Parker-Pearson, reports from the Stonehenge Riverside Project's research,

> The Durrington Avenue ran from the riverside to the Southern Circle, a distance of just over 186 yards.[1] Its width is comparable to the Stonehenge Avenue although it is much shorter. This avenue met the river at approximately the same point as today, culminating in a steep drop down the chalk river cliff to the water. The Durrington Avenue and Southern Circle were the main components of a ceremonial complex that was at the centre of a very large settlement whose house floors are well preserved. (12)

In addition, nearer to Stonehenge, about 1.2 miles (2km) to the northeast, there was another sacred site, called Woodhenge. It was originally constructed of a series of concentric circles of wooden poles placed within a circular bank and ditch. The ditch surrounding this was roughly circular with a diameter of about 94 yards [2] and it had a single entrance, and a causeway oriented to the Northeast. So it was oriented to the midsummer sunrise, like Stonehenge.

---

[1] = 170m
[2] = 86m

It was a circular temple of similar size to Stonehenge. Archaeologists date its construction to about 2,250 BC. With a processional avenue leading from the temple to the river, it is clear that it was designed as a sacred processional way. It is very likely that sacred processions took place from these sites, along the Avenue, and that these involved rituals for the Dead, but were also timed to occur at key seasonal rituals, especially at the summer and winter solstice times.

Cursus and Avenue: partly a site for the Dead
Less than half a mile (.8km) to the north of Stonehenge there is one of those remarkable and huge features made by the Megalithic people, called a cursus. Cursus is a Latin word for a course, which we would normally refer to as a course-way. This feature is a long, straight strip of land that has been created by digging out a shallow trench in the limestone, creating a white walled embankment. The excavated soil was placed on the course-way, and all vegetation was removed from the long rectangular site.

The Stonehenge Cursus was built about 3,300 BC, some centuries before Stonehenge and extends for a mile. It was in effect an inaccessible straight strip of land obviously used for ceremonial purposes. There was also a smaller cursus near Stonehenge, but excavation of this 400 metre-long Lesser Cursus suggested that some of its ditches were filled almost immediately after being dug.

The longest cursus in all of Britain, the Dorset Cursus near Blandford, is about six miles long (9.75km). As John Wood points out,

> All 10 of the 10 long barrows within sight of the Stonehenge Cursus are aligned on either the western end or the eastern end of the cursus that proves that these long barrows post-date the building of the cursus. Therefore, it was the building of the cursus that prompted the subsequent positioning of these long barrows. From the centre of the cursus, there is a

terminal which is a carefully levelled platform that acts as an observatory for sightings of the moon on the horizon. The cursus provides sightlines for the moon at minor and major standstill points in its nineteen-year cycle. (10)

The lunar standstills are an intriguing phenomenon, bringing with them an intensifying and then rapidly, a weakening lunar influence. These lunar cycles feature very prominently in the alignments of Stonehenge itself. As Richard Mudhar states,

> "The cursus was a ditch hewn in the chalk a couple of metres deep and wide. This would have appeared brilliant white in the green of what had now become pastureland. The hunter-gatherers of the totem pole had given way to farmers, who stayed long enough in one region to construct large earthworks." (13)

There is also the very extensive processional Way, called the Stonehenge Avenue, which commences from the Heel Stone, and proceeds down to the Avon River. The Avenue is nearly 2 miles (3.2km) long, and is often 300 yards (274m) wide. So, Stonehenge was constructed in an area that was a prominent sacred site for the Megalithic people, but unlike the buildings of Durrington Walls, and the wooden temple at Woodhenge, Stonehenge survived for millennia, as stone uprights were used, instead of timber poles.

Timberhenge, Bluestone henge
And in addition another stone circle has been found, nearer to the Avon River and constructed entirely of the special bluestones which were brought all the way from Wales. This is referred to as Bluestone Henge.[3] The outer henge here was constructed about 2,400 BC, but other parts were probably constructed 500 years earlier.

---

[3] If the bluestones inside Stonehenge were used for healing rituals, and this is not known, this complete bluestone circle would have been used as a dedicated healing temple.

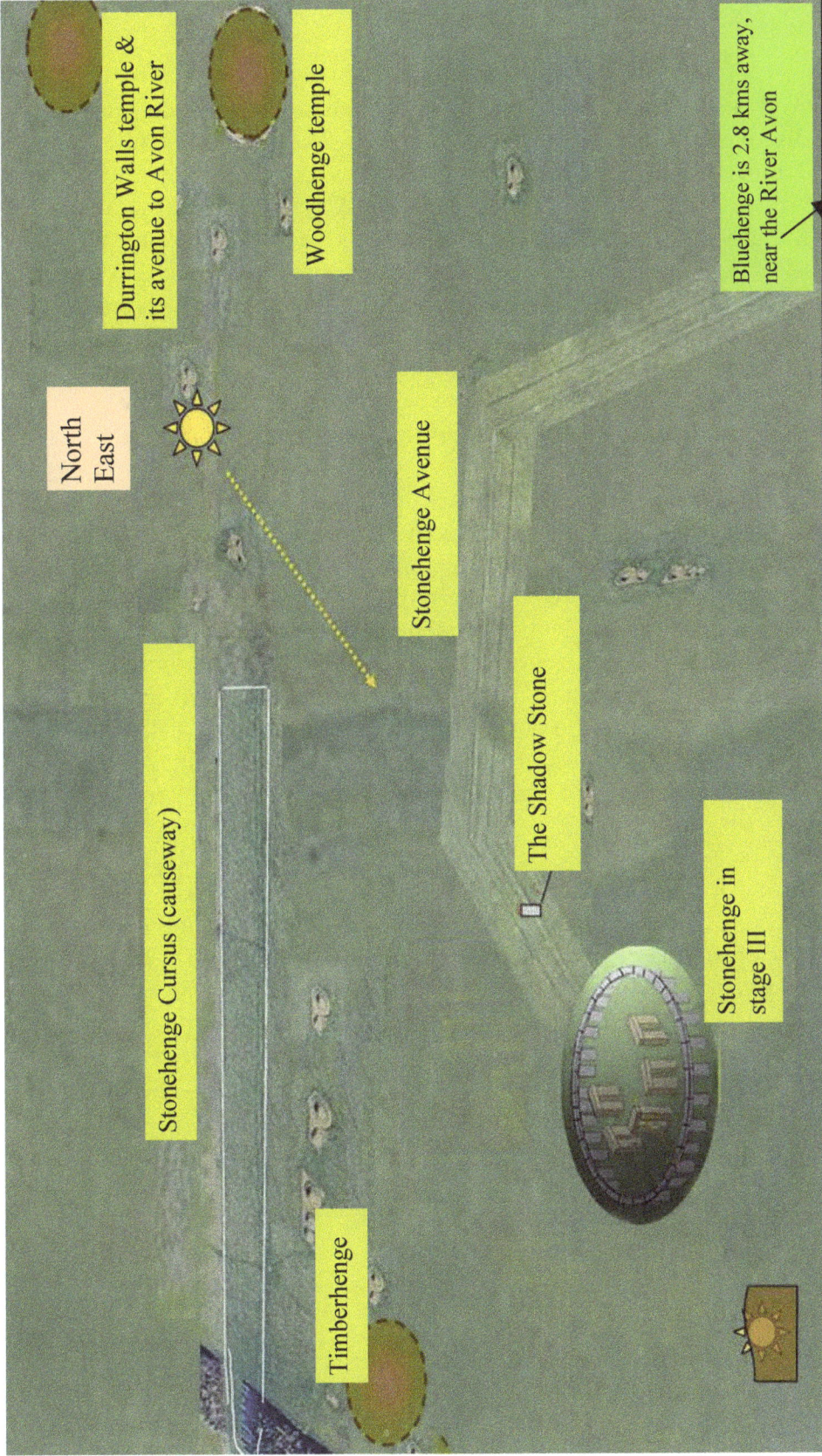

Durrington Walls temple & its avenue to Avon River

Woodhenge temple

North East

Stonehenge Avenue

Bluehenge is 2.8 kms away, near the River Avon

Stonehenge Cursus (causeway)

The Shadow Stone

Stonehenge in stage III

Timberhenge

1 An overview of Salisbury Plains about 2000 BC. Stonehenge was the grandest of the various temples and features in the area.

And also just 900m away from Stonehenge, evidence was discovered in 2010 of a wooden circle now called Timberhenge, built perhaps 4,500 years ago. It is the same size as Stonehenge, but today there only remain some pits in the ground where the large timber posts once stood, it seems to have been comprised of 24 posts originally. So it is now clear that Stonehenge was one sacred site amongst several other sacred sites in a large complex. However, Stonehenge was a much more sophisticated site than any of the others, and would have required much more skill to construct, and placed far more demands on the builders, and over many more years.

We also need to note in passing that just 16 miles to the north of Stonehenge is to be found another very significant group of sites erected by the Megalithic people. Firstly there is the Avebury henge, which is a complex of two huge henges, covering 28 acres, with a sarsen circle that once had 100 uprights. It is now occupied by a village, and is therefore of course, no longer intact. There is also the massive, artificially made Silbury Hill, the largest such mound in Europe, rising to 130 ft (40m) and covering 5.5 acres, and consisting of a million cubic yards of chalkstone. Its purpose is unknown.

The work involved in creating Silbury Hill may have even exceeded that required to create Stonehenge, although Stonehenge is of much greater technical complexity. There is also Windhill Hill, which is a truly massive long barrow, some 350 ft (107m) in length. Finally, in this area is the West Kennett long barrow, a burial site some 60 ft long (18m) and 35 ft wide (10.6m) and with five tomb chambers. (14) So the builders of Stonehenge chose a site which was the most extensive sacred site-complex of the Megalithic people, and had already become a sacred site centuries, even millennia earlier.

Chapter Three: The changing designs and use of Stonehenge

Stonehenge: its design in Stage One

The actual process whereby Stonehenge was built occurred over some 2,000 years, during which time it was altered and expanded. But all explanations of the construction phases are somewhat imprecise, because the exact situation is very hard to determine so long after the events. The soft chalk soil landscape has been substantially affected over the millennia by animal activity and climatic factors. The reader will find therefore varying accounts of how it was built. We will now try to give what seems to be the most accepted and accurate account of its construction.

The First Stage of Stonehenge began about 3,000 BC, when on the open grassland, on the limestone soil of the Salisbury Plains, a circular enclosure was made by digging two banks and a ditch. The outer circle made of the rubble from the ditch, was about 380 feet in diameter (116m), and had a single entrance to the northeast. It was about 8ft wide (2.4m) with a quarry ditch of 1.5 to 2 yards deep (1.3 - 1.8m). Then, some 35 ft (or 10.6 metres) inside this outer ring, beyond the ditch, is the inner bank, about 6ft high, and some 20 ft wide, and made of chalk soil, this inner ring had a diameter of 320 ft [4]. The outer embankment has all but disappeared today. Already here we meet a special feature of Stonehenge; the quarry ditch was outside the chalk bank, instead of being inside this embankment.

A circle of 56 holes, known as the Aubrey holes, was dug around the perimeter of this circle, just inside the edge of the circular raised bank. They were named after a 17th century antiquarian, John Aubrey, who discovered them. Some archaeological evidence has been found to suggest that these were filled in some centuries after being made; but this is not

---

[4] = That is, 1.8m high x 6m wide & 97.5m in diameter.

definite. The holes themselves vary in size, from 2.5 to and 3.5 feet,[5] and they have a depth between 2 and 4 feet.[6] The holes are not in a perfect circle; some are almost two feet off of the proper diameter or distance along the circle for an exact even spacing. But some centuries after being formed, cremated remains were put in about 25 of these holes, indicating that they were used later as a burial place.

It appears also that later in this same First Phase, a simple wooden structure was built inside this circle, or at least a cluster of wooden poles were set up in a roughly circular shape. In fact, it is believed that this wooden structure was of a similar shape to the stone sarsen circles that were erected much later. (16) In addition to this, about 40 wooden posts were erected just outside the raised bank for detailed monitoring of the moon's motions, in particular the lunar node cycle of 18.6 years; we shall explore what this is, later. It also appears that there were some wooden posts at the southern entrance to the henge, as well. Then, over the centuries, stone was favoured over wood, and four menhirs, or upright stones, were placed on the edge of the circle.

Two gateway stones were placed at the entry to the circular bank, and outside this, the so-called "Heel Stone", of hard sandstone, was raised. This is a large un-worked sarsen stone, which now lies next to the A344 road. It was erected outside the north-eastern entrance to the circle. This stone was aligned to the summer solstice sunrise, so the sun could be seen as it rises, moving up the left side of this stone, when viewed from a point in the centre of the circle. As Christiaan reports (17):

> The naturally shaped Heel Stone is about 20 feet long and 8 feet wide by 7 feet thick.[7] Its lower 4 feet is buried in the ground and it weighs an estimated 35 tons. It is made up of natural sandstone called sarsen which is thought to have come from Marlborough

---

[5] = 0.76m to 1.07m
[6] = 0.6m and 1.2m
[7] = 6.1 m long and 2.4 m wide by 2.1 m thick

Downs, 20 miles to the north of Stonehenge. Currently the heel stone leans inward toward the circle at an angle of about 30 degrees from the perpendicular, but it is believed that the stone was once standing straight. Circling the stone about 12 feet from its base is a covered ditch filled with chalk. (http://www.christiaan.com/stonehenge/index.)

On the summer solstice day, June 21st or 22nd, the rising sun slowly moves up the length of the rock, creating a shadow that extends deep into the circle of sarsen rocks, which in fact are opened towards the rising sun, by having a horseshoe shape that opens up towards the northeast. So, in Stage One the site was aligned with the midsummer sunrise and the midwinter sunset, and the most southerly rising and northerly setting of the moon. In addition, the remarkable Aubrey holes had been created for observation of eclipses. We shall explore what these astronomical events are, and how Stonehenge is aligned to them, later. Now let's see how Stonehenge was developed further in its next stage.

Stonehenge: its design in Stage Two
About 2,000 BC Stonehenge entered its Second Stage, when more complex features were added, see illustration 4. The two stones at the entrance to the complex were removed. In the centre of the circular raised bank, work began on setting up two rings of bluestones (or more accurately, arcs of bluestones, because the rings were not finished). Unlike the other sarsen stones which were sourced locally, these bluestones were brought in from western Wales, about 213kms (132 miles) away! We shall explore the question of how this was done, below. The stones are not actually blue, but grey-brown; although when wet, they appear to have a bluish tinge. These stones are not a special type of rock, but encompass a variety of rocks. An excellent website providing detailed, reliable information on Stonehenge tells us:

"The stones, which weighed about 4 tons, consisted mostly of spotted dolerite but included examples of rhyolite, tuff and volcanic and calcareous ash. Each measures around 6.5 ft in height, between 3ft and 5 ft wide and around 2.6 ft thick.[8] Amongst these was a six ton specimen of green micaceous sandstone, twice the height of the bluestones, and it was to become known as the Altar Stone, a rectangular pillar about 16 ft (4.9m) in length." (18)

The Altar Stone may have stood as a single large monolith near the centre of the circle, and though it is usually considered to have been upright, it may also have been recumbent, and never vertical. One reason it is unlikely to have been upright is that it would have been in the way of the line-of-sight. Also it appears to be aligned to the centre of the circle; yet if it had fallen over, it would very likely have fallen out of alignment to its original position. The north-eastern entrance was also widened at this time with the result that it precisely matched the direction of the midsummer sunrise and midwinter sunset of the period.

It was at this stage in all probability that the four important stones were erected, known as the so-called Station Stones; these took the shape of a rectangle. They enabled observation of the rising and setting of both the moon and sun at key times of the year. They also enabled a more detailed observation of the Moon's movements, especially of what is called its major still-stands (see below). It is often said that these Station Stones were not placed in their sites until Stage Three, but this statement is unlikely to be accurate, as they are the key stones for the observation of both solar and lunar cycles, which is a major purpose of Stonehenge in Stage Two.

It is true that they were not already placed in Stage One, because as Castelden points out, the socket of one of them (no. 94) was cut right through into one of the Aubrey Holes, which therefore must have existed already. (19) And as Hawkins mentioned, the rubble from the mounds dug out around them

---

[8] = 2m in height, between .9m and 1.5m wide and around 0.8m

overlies those of earlier earthworks. (20) But they were not set up as late as Stage Three, as the great circle of sarsens would have blocked their line of sight. So the Station Stones were set up in Stage Two, or they may have been set up at some intermediate time between Stage One and Stage Two.

Two more uprights were placed outside the circle, near the Heel Stone, allowing more accurate confirmation of the summer solstice sunrise than previously. Of these only one now remains; it has fallen over. This is the so-called the Slaughter Stone, which is 16 ft long (4.9 m). It gained its name from a mistaken attitude that it was purposely in the horizontal plane for slaughtering victims, in cruel Druid rituals. Various Roman texts have declared the Druids to be involved in such rituals, but the actual facts about the Druids are hard to ascertain.

The Romans had political reasons to denigrate their enemy. Also in this Stage, circular ditches were dug around the Heel Stone, and around two of the four Station Stones also, the reason for these is unknown. In addition it was during Stage One that the Stonehenge Avenue was constructed; a straight line of parallel ditches, at this stage, 560 metres long, forming a sort of processional way. The Avenue was extended much further, in a later stage.

Stonehenge: its design in Stage Three
The site was developed further about a century later, probably about 1,900 BC. The two aligned stones near the Heel Stone or Cover Stone were removed, and two stones were put at the entrance to the complex. The two incomplete circles of bluestones from Phase 2, (these had never been completed), were removed, and two rings of sarsen stones were set up instead. The sarsen stones came from about 24 miles away (39 km) from a quarry on Marlborough Downs. We noted earlier that Stonehenge had been constructed as if it were of wood, using carpentry techniques:

The stones were dressed and fashioned with mortise and tenon joints before 30 were erected as a 108 ft [9] diameter circle of standing stones with a lintel of 30 stones resting on top. The lintels themselves were joined to one another using another woodworking method, the tongue-in-groove joint. Each stone weighed around 25 tons and had clearly been worked with the final effect in mind.... The sides of the stones that face inwards are more finely worked than the sides that face outwards. A total of 74 stones would have been needed to complete the circle and unless some of the sarsens were removed from the site, it would seem that the ring was left incomplete. (21)

So, the outermost stone circle consists of 30 upright sarsens of which 17 still stand, each weighs about 25 tons. The outer sarsen circle is one hundred feet (30.5m) in diameter. Each stone is about 13.5 ft high and 7ft wide. [10] The space between each of the stones is approximately four feet (1.2m). These were put in a carefully spaced circle around a ring of five sets of trilithon sarsen stones in the centre of the site. These stones were in fact placed a little more to the east than the earlier bluestone arcs, giving the site an orientation to the northeast, and hence lined up with the NE avenue. (22) One can see that a huge amount of work was needed by many people to create such a monument; one estimate is that the construction of original structure required 1.5 million man-days of physical labour to do this.

Professor Atkinson, the primary archaeological expert on Stonehenge in the last century, estimated that with no less than 1,500 men working constantly, with only a few days of rest between trips, it would have taken five and a half years to move the sarsen stones from the nearby Avebury hills to Stonehenge! There is also the immense work of chipping away at the sarsen stones, removing small quantities

---

[9] = 33m
[10] = That is, 4.11m high x 2.13m wide.

laboriously, to shape them into the required form. Atkinson also estimates that the labour involved in this task required removing some 3 million cubic inches of stone and would have taken a million man-hours to carry out. This inner ring has a horseshoe shape and consisted of five sets of trilithons, a Greek word which means three-stones, i.e., two uprights with a horizontal cap:

> "These huge stones, ten uprights and five lintels, weigh up to 50 tons each and were again linked using complex jointings. The images of a dagger and 14 axe-heads have been recorded carved on one of the sarsens, known as stone 53. Further axe-head carvings have been seen on the outer faces of stones known as numbers 3, 4, and 5." (17)

Stage Three B

Finally in the last phase, work began on erecting two new circles of bluestones, this time outside the sarsen rings. The holes were dug for them, but this plan was abandoned for unknown reasons and instead, inside the outer ring of sarsen stones, a circle of small bluestones was set up. The bluestone circle is about 75 ft (22.8m) in diameter. Most of the stones have at first a height of 6.5 ft (2m), but they increase in size moving towards the south-west, reaching a maximum of 8 ft (2.44m).

The stones have a width between 3 and 4 ft (0.9 -1.22m). There are 19 of these bluestones: this is very significant, as we shall later see, because 19 years (or precisely 18.6) is a key lunar number. In addition, a small number of bluestones were set up in an oval or horse-shoe shape at the heart of the circle, inside the inner sarsen trilithon. Then a small amount of the bluestones forming this circle were removed, creating another horse-shoe pattern.

Today, few of these remain. Of the original nineteen stones, only six are still in place. Significantly, of those sarsens that remain, a few have cuts in them like timber working cuts, suggesting they may have been linked with lintels and part of a larger structure during this phase. (17) At this time, the so-called Altar Stone may have been set up in the centre of the whole arrangement. In addition, around the outer circle of sarsens, two circles of holes were dug, called the Z and the Y holes. These were never used, and gradually filled with soil over the centuries. Various theories about their purpose are in circulation, but nothing can be found to substantiate these.

But they are intriguing because, as Hawkins mentions, they are irregularly spaced yet the builders were capable of very precise work! Secondly, they were filled with a fine soil, not the usual coarse rubble. Moreover, nearly all of these holes had one single piece of bluestone put into it! In this phase too, the Avenue, which we noted was begun in Stage Two, was further lengthened. It consisted of twin banks about 12m (39ft) apart with internal ditches, and begins at the entrance to the embankment. Now it was extended, and changed direction, becoming 1.5 mile (2.4 km) in length, going to the Avon River.

The vast work and remarkable skills involved
With regard to the carving of the sarsens, really skilled work was called for, to ensure that the standing stones and their capstones would be held securely in place,

> These giant sandstones, or sarsen stones as they are now called, were hammered to size and shaped using balls of stone known as mauls. Even today you can see the drag marks. Each pair of stones was heaved upright and linked on the top by the lintels. To get the lintels to stay in place, they made joints in the stones, linking the lintels in a circular manner using a tongue and groove joint, and subsequently the upright and lintel with a ball and socket joint, or mortice and tenon. This was all cleverly designed on the alignment of the rising of the summer solstice sun and the setting of the winter solstice sun. (17)

How were these huge stones really transported to the site? They are massive, some weighing 50 tons. No one can say for sure, although various ingenious theories have been put forward. One suggestion is that they were put on wooden tree-trunk rollers and hauled with leather ropes. But others have argued that the sheer weight of these massive stones would have crushed the wooden tree trunks being used. Another theory is that they were all encased in some soft material, and rolled all the way to the site.

The most likely theory is that they were placed on wooden sleds and these were, in turn, placed on wooden tracks, which were lubricated with animal fat. It is thought that the stones were actually raised into position on the site by digging holes, sliding them into these, and using some sort of system of pulley ropes to haul them upright. A similar system based on sheer manpower is thought to have been used to raise the heavy lintels or horizontal slabs onto the upright stones.

Another point about these sarsens is the degree of artistic or rather architectural awareness that they reveal. It might look as if they have a straight edge, but in fact they actually have a slight convex taper. This shaping of them counteracts the foreshortening effect which you naturally get, from looking up at them from the ground. In other words, to the observer, they appear to be as wide at the top as at the bottom. (23)

It is also the case that "the lintel stones curve slightly to continue the circular appearance of the earlier monument." (18) All of this indicates that, in great contrast to every other stone circle in Britain, a tremendously advanced architectural project was undertaken, with skills derived from carpentry and experienced temple building, such as we associate with ancient Greece.

It is difficult to determine how the sarsens were transported from a place not so far away. But if the amount of work involved in transporting them is astonishing, then the mystery of how they transported the Welsh bluestones is even greater.

As we noted earlier, geologists have determined that these stones came from the Prescelli Mountains in Pembroke, South Wales, 140 miles (225km) away.

And such is the sheer effort involved in bringing such stones from this distance, that various legendary explanations have been created in old English literature. These legends refer to a magical power of Merlin through which he effectively reduced their weight. But even considering him to be an historical figure, he could have nothing to do with the bluestones, as his era was much later than early Stonehenge. However he can be seen as representing the highest ranking priest of the Megalithic Wessex people, who was in charge of the project.

One academic source, the Western Washington University Planetarium, suggests the stones were put on wooden tree-trunk rollers and hauled with leather ropes,

> They were perhaps dragged on rollers and sledges to the headwaters on Milford Haven, and then loaded onto rafts. Placed on a raft, a large mass is relatively easy to transport. The rafts could have travelled by water along the south coast of Wales and up the rivers Avon and Frome, before being dragged overland again to near Warminster in Wiltshire. The final stage of the journey was mainly by water, down the river Wyley to Salisbury, then the Salisbury Avon to west Amesbury. The journey covers nearly 240 miles. It was an amazing feat when you consider that each stone weighs about five tons. (24)

However, there are many who find this explanation improbable, since rivers and valleys and hills would all have to be negotiated. Some have concluded that a special kind of engineering technique, unknown today, was used. Others have considered the possibility of some kind of energy, similar to the Ch'i of the Chinese or the Prana of the Indians; an energy which is not known in the modern Western world. That is, an energy source which reduced the weight of the stones.

People who incline towards this explanation mention legends or supposedly true reports from travellers in previous centuries, suggesting that shamanistic priests did have access to such energies. These legends may be entirely fanciful, but curiously they often refer to the use of sound, and modern scientists are able to produce modest anti-gravity effects by using ultra-sonic sound energy. Japanese science laboratories in particular continue to pursue this phenomenon in the hope of making it viable.[11]

Could such alternative theories which suggest that the ancients may have been able to reduce the weight of large rock slabs, (not only in Salisbury but elsewhere in the ancient world), possibly have merit? The answer remains unknown, and the divide between modern rationalist science and an assumed quasi-magical power of priests of old times is obviously huge. However it was actually done, the process of building Stonehenge was a hugely demanding one.

Why the Bluestones were used
Why did the builders use bluestones from far away Wales? One theory is that these stones were ancestral memory stones, reminding the Wessex people of their ancestors, for the theory suggests that these ancestors came from Wales. This is a very unlikely idea, with no firm basis to it. A more likely theory is from two scientists, Professor Tim Darvill, of the University of Bournemouth, and Professor Geoff Wainwright, of the Society of Antiquaries. These men suggest that the stones come from a site where healing was offered by the priest or medicine man of the Megalithic people, perhaps in the form of rituals.

It has been known that a significant proportion of the newly discovered Neolithic remains at Stonehenge show clearly that they had been wounded, showing signs of operations to their skull, or had walked with a limp, or had broken bones. It has

---

[11] See for example, the science article in *Sensors and Actuators, Physical* vol.1, "*A non-contact linear bearing and actuator via ultra-sonic levitation*", by T. Ide, J. Friend, K. Nakamura, S.Euha, April 2007.

been established that many of these people had travelled long distances to get to Stonehenge in southwest England. This indicates that they were seeking supernatural or spiritual help for their medical conditions. It is intriguing that Geoffrey of Monmouth in the twelfth century described the bluestones as possessing healing properties. The BBC reported on a new archaeological dig being undertaken at Stonehenge by these two scientists, in order to determine the accuracy of their theory:

> Darvill and Wainwright have traced the bluestones - the stones in the centre of Stonehenge - to the exact spot they came from in the Preseli hills, 140 miles away in the far west of Wales. Neolithic inscriptions found at this location indicate the ancient people there believed the stones to be magical and for the local waters to have healing properties. Darvill and Wainwright hope the dig will demonstrate such beliefs also lay behind the creation of Stonehenge, by showing that the make-up of the original floor of the sacred circle at the monument is dominated by bluestone chippings that were purposely placed there. (25)

So what is the answer? We believe that this really interesting theory is only partly correct. So what is the situation?

Firstly, the stones came from the Prescelli Mountains of Wales. But very significantly, this is an area which was sacred to the ancient Britons. In the Prescelli Mountains there is evidence of extensive Megalithic cultic activity. [12] This includes stone-circles such as Gors Fawr and spiritual observation sites such as Pentre-Ifan; these are what we call shadow-chambers, see below about them. For example see, http://www.ancient-wisdom.co.uk/

---

[12] Curiously the earliest references to King Arthur, the greatest mythical hero of England, and thus to the greatest sacred site in the land, come from ancient Welsh literature.

And there are also dolmens and tombs oriented to the solstice or equinox sunrise. It is very likely that this prominent sacred site in Wales was venerated before Stonehenge was planned. And this tells us why the bluestones were of such high priority that they were transported all the way to Stonehenge.

To incorporate stones from that older, venerated site was very important, because their presence on the Wiltshire plains bestowed a kind of consecration on the magnificent, uniquely complex site. This greatest of all Megalithic projects, Stonehenge, was given a validity and a sanctity by the use of the Prescelli bluestones.

Perhaps also to the mind-set of the ancient Britons, these stones were regarded as holding sacred energies, absorbed from their location in the sacred site in the Welsh mountains. And as a consequence of this, it may well have been believed that these bluestones also had healing powers. In any event, the new site of Stonehenge would have strengthened its status by incorporating such stones. We note in passing that some writers on Stonehenge have argued that these stones had been transported to the area from Wales by the action of glaciers, long before the Megalithic people built Stonehenge. But this idea has not received much scientific support, mainly because lots of other rocks, of smaller size should also have been found on the Salisbury Plains to support this theory, but this is not the case.

The Slaughter Stone
A prominent fallen stone is called the Slaughter Stone. As we mentioned earlier there is no historical proof of any slaughter of people being carried out by Druids in their rituals. It was probably a slanderous report created by the Romans to justify their aggressive wars against another nation. It was not clear what made this stone topple, but it is clear that its red discolouration is due to iron pigment in the rock having being subject to rain over many years. It is not due to blood stains. It

has also been subject to much destruction over the centuries. As one website reports;

> During WW1, a track way passing through Stonehenge was being set up, and later archaeological research discovered holes drilled across the corner of the stone. But given the harsh conditions, which it was made to undergo, it is indeed a miracle that it survived till this day. (26)

Chapter Four: Stonehenge and its Alignments

Monitoring celestial & seasonal energies

It is indisputable that Stonehenge has astronomical orientations; we briefly noted this when considering the stages by which Stonehenge was constructed. Despite the traditional view of mainstream archaeology in the 1970's, this cosmic feature of Stonehenge, and indeed all Megalithic sites including many Neolithic tombs, became a self-evident fact. The original breakthrough in realizing that Stonehenge does have a many-sided relationship to the cosmos through its alignments, came about through the pioneering work of a Boston University astronomer, Dr. Gerald Hawkins in the 1960's.

Hawkins' work established that the Megalithic people built their monuments with various alignments to the heavens. There were some errors in Hawkins' book, because the map of Stonehenge that he used was imperfect, so Hawkins' conclusions were not at first widely accepted by many astronomers. However, eminent astronomer Sir Fred Hoyle, the Astronomer Royal, stepped into the emotive debate and confirmed that the major alignments discovered by Hawkins are indeed correct (but not other lesser ones). In 1965 Hoyle revised and corrected Hawkins' work, and also revised Hawkins' method for predicting eclipses.

Hoyle's method is more accurate than Hawkins, because the actual day of the eclipse can be predicted, as well as the season of the eclipse. Today these discoveries are generally accepted as proven facts. These key alignments have been pivotal in establishing that the Megalithic people in building Stonehenge were aligning it to certain astronomical phenomena. The core discoveries of Hawkins were affirmed again by an amateur, but very experienced British astronomer, A. C. Newham in his small booklet, "The Astronomical Significance of Stonehenge".

These days many academics as well as reputable astronomical societies around the world have confirmed that these alignments are factual. But this fact is only accepted to a limited degree in mainstream archaeology, where there is still strong reluctance to acknowledge this striking aspect to Stonehenge. For example, in recent times, Prof. John North has undertaken extensive research to show precisely the alignments to celestial points of many burial sites in the UK, but his conclusions about Stonehenge's own alignments are similar to those mainstream archaeologists. Later we shall see just why the archaeological world is sceptical about the astronomical side of Stonehenge.

Lets now explore this theme of alignments, to see exactly what these alignments are, and then we can explore why they were so important to the builders of Stonehenge. Now, as a new contribution to research about Stonehenge, we are going to suggest that the lines-of-sight of Stonehenge are part of its special features. A further part of Stonehenge are the shadow-fields created by those huge stone uprights.

The lines-of-sight at Stonehenge in Stages I & II
In Stage One, the four Station Stones together with the so-called Heel Stone, allowed several key facts of the seasonal cycle to be identified. The key astronomical fact is that the summer solstice (June 21st or 22nd), the longest day of the year, could be identified by the rising of the sun almost directly above the Heel Stone. It is the most famous aspect of Stonehenge that, as the sun appears over the horizon on this day, it can be seen rising up above the Heel Stone: an obvious focus on the solar aspect. (We shall examine later the fact that it actually does not appear precisely above this stone.)

This alignment of the Heel Stone with its two accompanying gateway stones also meant that, by looking in the evening of that day, in exactly the opposite direction, the winter solstice sunset position could be identified as well. This event marks the beginning of the longest night of the year.

The second key astronomical event that could be observed is a really special astronomical feature; it is the so-called major and minor Standstill of the moon. The standstill refers to the phenomenon that happens each time when, the moon reaches a peak of its orbital path around the Earth. This occurs every 18.6 years.

The moon then rises and sets in extreme points on the horizon, much further to the north and also to the south, than is usual. This is a feature in the lunar cycle that was known only in a theoretical way to modern astronomers. So, what is this phenomenon of which we modern people are so unaware, and which to the Megalithic people was so important?

Lunar Standstills: what are they?
The lunar standstill is the event where the position of the moon, relative to the sun, changes dramatically. The moon is seen coming up over the horizon much further to the north, and then rising up higher in the sky (i.e., nearer to the zenith or overhead point) than the sun would, even if it were the summertime. But that's not all; two weeks later, the moon is seen coming up over the horizon much further to the south, and then only going up very low in the sky. It moves across the sky even lower than sun would go if it were the cold winter days. So it rises very high up in the sky, and then a fortnight later, goes very low across the sky.

A major standstill occurs when the moon is at this extreme difference to its usual path. At this time, people looking into the sky will see the moon moving across the heavens higher than the sun goes in the summer, but then only two weeks later, it will be seen moving across the sky lower than the sun's path, even in the wintertime. In other words, a major standstill occurs when each end of the moon's orbital plane has its most pronounced tilt. Its upper end will be tilted up the highest it can be, and the other end will be tilted down below the sun's orbital plane as far down as it can be. Firstly, illustration 2 shows the orbital path of the moon and the sun, as these two bodies (apparently) orbit around the Earth.

The orbit or orbital path of both the sun and the moon could each be visualized as an oval tabletop; and these two tabletops intersect each other. The moon's orbital plane (the tabletop) is at an angle to that of the sun's orbital plane; it rises higher up on one end, and therefore sinks down below at the other end. But the moon's orbital plane does not stay fixed, it actually slowly rises and falls, like the tides, eventually getting to a 5° difference in its angle of incline, from that of the sun's orbital plane. The two points where these two imaginary tabletops meet are called the lunar nodes.

Now when a major standstill happens the moon, as it orbits around, comes to the tilted-up part, and then it comes to the tilted-down end two weeks later. So it undergoes extreme high and low risings over about two years, these gradually lessen in this period. So this situation is at its most noticeable for the viewer for quite some months, before it starts to return to its normal motions. Hence during this time it seems to the viewer that the moon stands still amidst its extreme motions.

Two weeks separate the highest positions from the lowest positions, because the moon takes 28 days to complete its circuit (the lunar month), and hence 14 days to move from the higher end to the lower. The moon takes 18 years and seven months (18.6 yrs) to complete this cycle; so the standstill is in effect an oscillation of the moon's orbital plane, of its intersection points (its nodes) with the orbital path to the sun, see illustration 3.

Here it is easy to graphically see what the lines-of-sight that Stonehenge, in its early times (Phases I & II) were designed to allow. From this diagram, one can visually appreciate that these extremes in the moon's positions, relative to the sun, were especially noted by the Megalithic people. We can note here the amazing fact about Stonehenge, in Stages I and II, that the summer solstice sunrise and lunar standstill actually

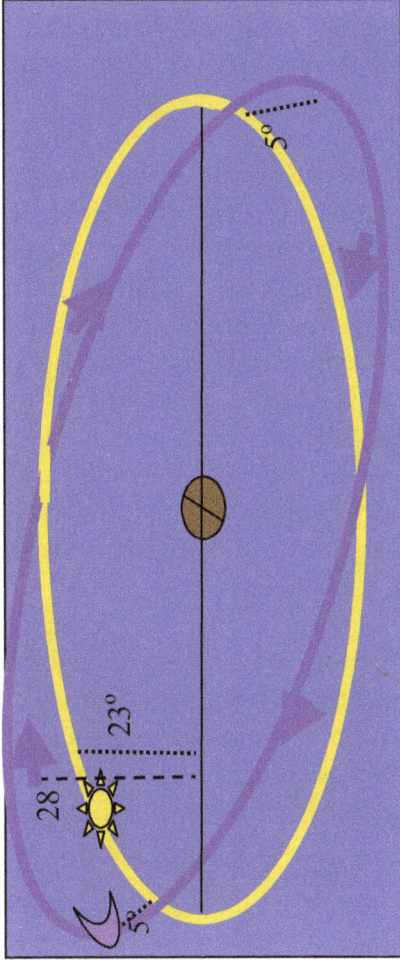

2   The MAJOR STANDSTILL

The orbital path of the moon & the sun, (a northern hemisphere focus.)

The orbits of sun and moon are like two oval table tops which intersect each other. But the moon's pathway slowly pivots (rises and falls) over 18.6 years. Here the full five degree maximum tilt is shown; its orbital path is then tilted at 28° from the equator, instead of the sun's constant 23°.

When this happens, an observer on Earth will see the moon rise up extremely high, far to the north, when the moon is at that side of its path which is tilted **up above** the sun's orbit. Then the moon will cross the sky even higher then sun does in midsummer. The moon's energies are very strong.

But two weeks later, the moon has travelled around to the other side of its orbital path, where it is below the sun's path. Now the observer will see the rising moon staying extremely low, and far to the south. The moon will now cross the sky even lower than the sun does in midwinter. The moon's energies are very weak.

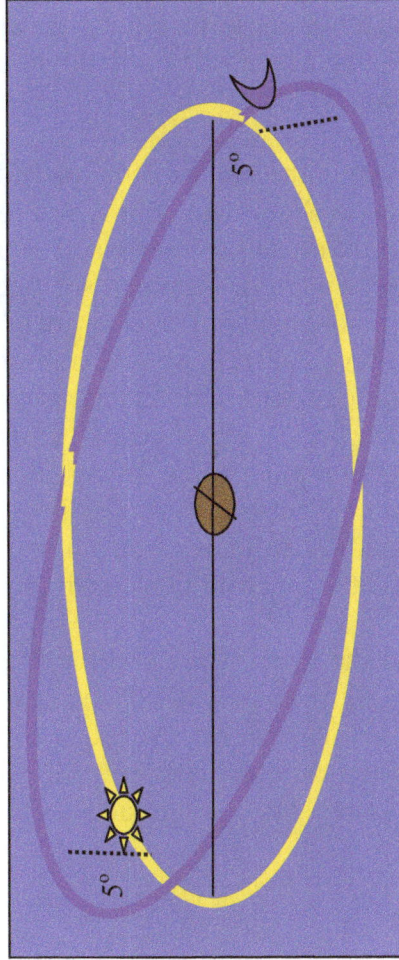

occur at right angles to each other. That is, the position on the horizon where the sun rises on the summer solstice and where the lunar major standstill occurs, are at right-angles to each other. But this is only true only if one is observing the sky from Stonehenge! The position of Stonehenge on the globe, namely at 51 degrees north, means that these two phenomena occur at right angles. So if Stonehenge had been built just 30 miles (48 km) to the south or north, then a right angle would not be formed between the position on the horizon where the Sun rises at the summer solstice, and the place in the heavens where the lunar standstill occurs.

Now, let's assess what the significance of all this is. Firstly, by choosing this latitude the builders could construct a right-angled observation site. That is a site in which they could position their stones exactly at right-angles to the solstice points, and in so doing, the Station Stones and later on the sarsen stones, would be in alignment with the lunar nodal points. Thereby they could monitor the activity going on in the heavens.

To find the precise location of the moon's nodal standstill is a very difficult task, but if you locate a sacred site at 51 degrees north, it can be determined more easily once you know where the winter or summer solstice sun will rise, because these special standstill events occur at right-angles to the solstice events. But this is only true at 51degrees latitude! And once you can determine key lunar and solar events, you can start to forecast when various celestial events will occur. For agricultural people living close to nature with farming and animal husbandry, this is a very important, empowering ability. But there is also a spiritual side to the seasonal cycle and the lunar influence, which we explore later.

So the Heel Stone, and the four Station Stones were designed to allow knowledge of the key seasonal events of the sun, and also the extreme events in the moon's cycle. In many early societies, especially the Megalithic people, the sun's annual journey was of great significance. It is the single most important factor regulating the planting of crops, for example. But in addition, this early stage of Stonehenge, with its 56 Aubrey holes enabled a very striking capability to monitor another aspect of the celestial bodies: the eclipses of the sun or the moon. Illustration 3 provides a really easy to visualize, graphic diagram of just what Stonehenge I & II were designed to observe.

The Aubrey Holes & the Lunar Node

In Stage I of Stonehenge a ring of holes known as the Aubrey holes were made. They were discovered during an exploration of the site in the mid 1600's, when John Aubrey discovered the remains of 56 even spaced holes that appeared to have been dug up and refilled many times over. These 56 holes were designed to enable the monitoring of the motion of the sun and moon, so as to be able to predict eclipses. Chris Whitcombe on his Earth Mysteries website, "Archeoastronomy at Stonehenge" writes:

> "For the archaeo-astronomists, the Aubrey Holes served as fixed reference points along a circle, and their number was essential to astronomical calculations. The cycle of the moon, for example, which takes 27.3 days, can be tracked by moving a marker by two holes each day to complete a circuit in 28 days. A much longer calculation is to move the marker by three holes per year to complete a full circuit in 18.67 years.

> In this way, it is argued, it would be possible to keep track of the nodes, points where the paths of the sun and the moon apparently intersect to produce an eclipse. Because the moon slews around in its path, the two nodes move along the path of the sun, a complete circuit of which takes 18.61 years. By means of the markers in the Aubrey Holes and keeping track of the directions of the sun and the moon, the astronomer at Stonehenge could calculate nodal points ahead of time and thus predict both lunar and solar eclipses." (27)

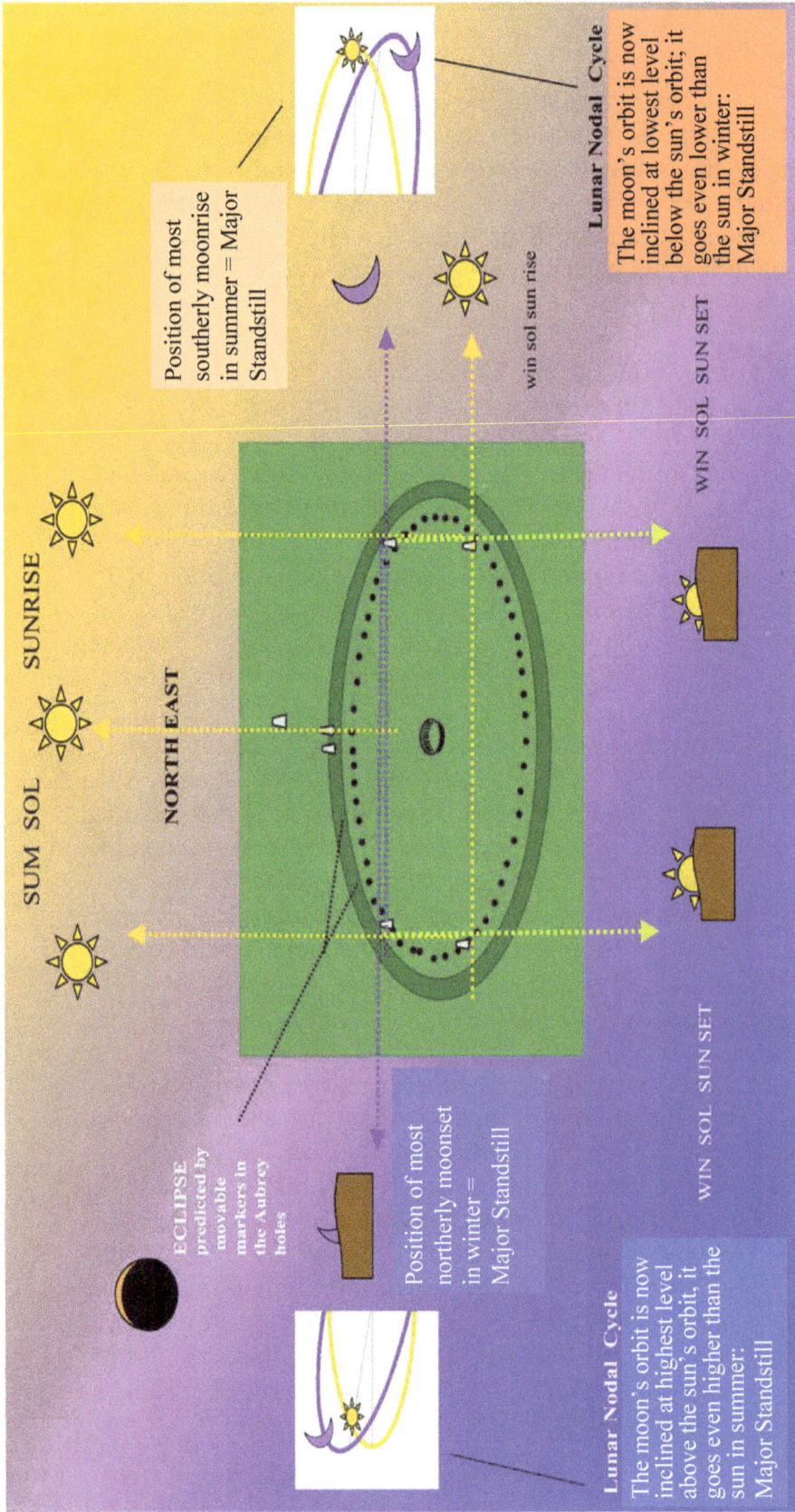

Position of most southerly moonrise in summer = Major Standstill

Lunar Nodal Cycle
The moon's orbit is now inclined at lowest level below the sun's orbit; it goes even lower than the sun in winter: Major Standstill

SUM SOL SUNRISE

NORTH EAST

win sol sun rise

WIN SOL SUN SET

WIN SOL SUN SET

ECLIPSE predicted by movable markers in the Aubrey holes

Position of most northerly moonset in winter = Major Standstill

Lunar Nodal Cycle
The moon's orbit is now inclined at highest level above the sun's orbit; it goes even higher than the sun in summer: Major Standstill

3 Stonehenge Stages 1 & 2: its lines of sight. The Heel Stone for summer Solstice / 4 Station Stones for lunar nodes / the 56 Aubrey Stones for predicting of eclipses.

46

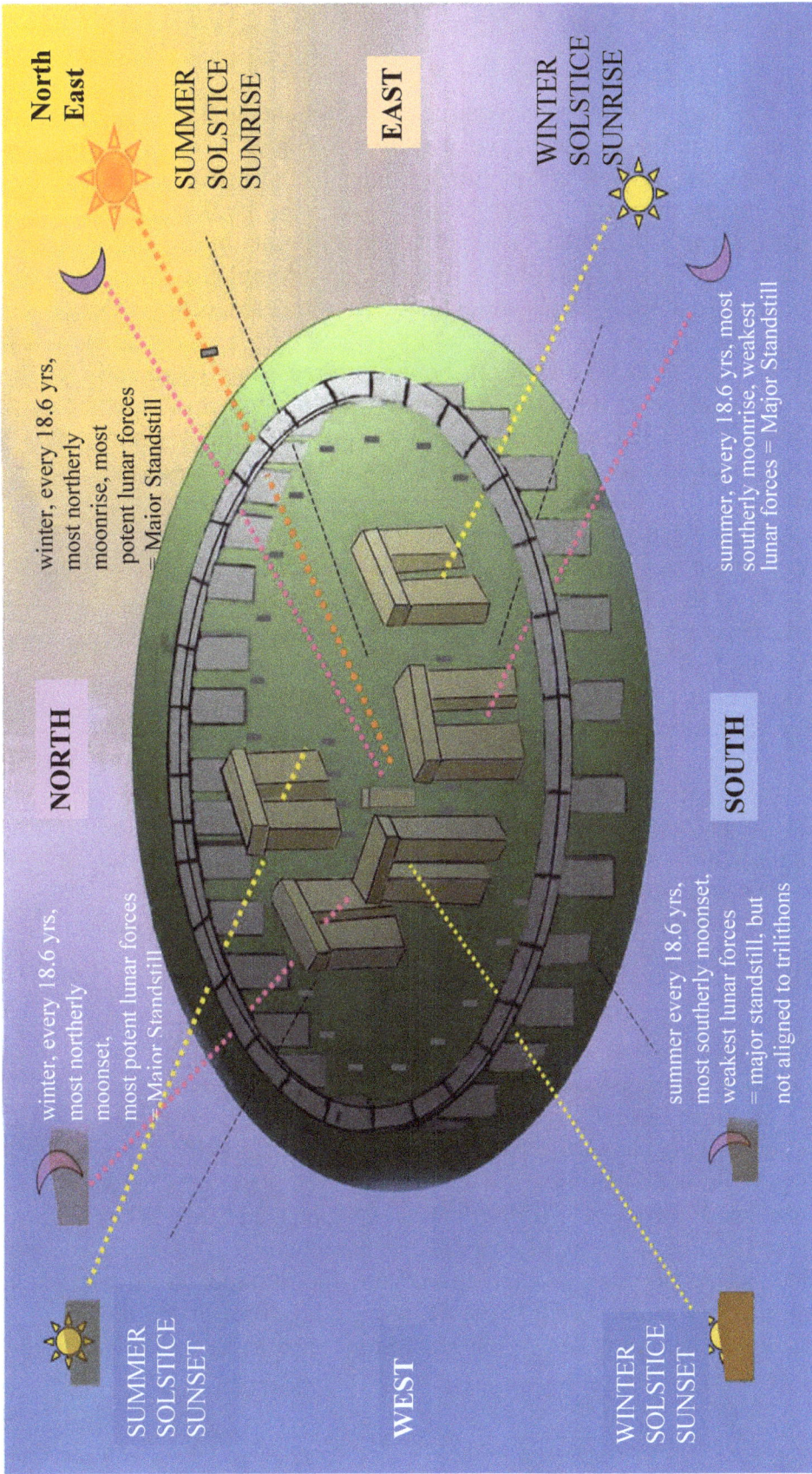

4 Stonehenge III: the lines of sight of the sarsens. The cosmic alignments of Stonehenge; the SW standstill moonset is not visible. Dashed lines represent the minor standstills.

North East

SUMMER SOLSTICE SUNRISE

EAST

WINTER SOLSTICE SUNRISE

NORTH

winter, every 18.6 yrs, most northerly moonrise, most potent lunar forces = Major Standstill

summer, every 18.6 yrs, most southerly moonrise, weakest lunar forces = Major Standstill

SOUTH

winter, every 18.6 yrs, most northerly moonset, most potent lunar forces = Major Standstill

summer every 18.6 yrs, most southerly moonset, weakest lunar forces = major standstill, but not aligned to trilithons

SUMMER SOLSTICE SUNSET

WEST

WINTER SOLSTICE SUNSET

So the Megalithic people constructed at Stonehenge in its first stage, a simple but effective way to predict eclipses, or in other words, a way to monitor the interrelated influences of the moon and sun. C.A. Newham, in his booklet, The Astronomical Significance of Stonehenge, points out that the number 56 is mathematically linked to the complex celestial motions of moon's nodes and the motion of the sun. (28)

There are 56 days' difference between three solar years and three lunar years, and hence 56 holes are needed or at least they are of value for a system of eclipse prediction, which extends of course far beyond a one year period. In view of this extraordinary calculation-device, we will need to consider later just what the eclipses meant on a spiritual level to the Megalithic people. The results of our exploration so far: the construction of Stonehenge in Stages I and II was intended to enable people to predict and experience the following:

A: the lunar nodes standstill phenomena
B: the summer solstice sunrise
C: winter solstice sunset, (and sunrise)
D: the predicting of eclipses of either sun or moon
E: In addition, a diagonal line-of-sight drawn through the Station Stones rectangle provides some alignment with the four main festival times of the Celtic, known as Quarter days; namely sunset in May (Beltane) and August (Lughnasa) and sunrise on February (Imbolc) and November (Samhain).

The lines-of-sight at Stonehenge in Stage III.
Look at illustration 4 to see clearly just what the later stages of Stonehenge actually enabled the priests to observe and monitor. This later stage is the one that we now identify as the classic Stonehenge circle (or circles) of upright sarsens, with its capped stones and trilithons. What has changed now? What does the line-of-sight of this classic Stonehenge offer to its priests? As we can readily appreciate, the summer solstice sunrise is still observed. It can be seen today from inside the sarsen circle, rising above the Heel Stone, just as in the early

stage of Stonehenge. The winter solstice sunset is also observable, but now the difference is that the highest of the trilithons is involved, this is known as the Grand Trilithon.

The last minutes of the sunset on the evening of the winter solstice signal the start of what later became known as the Yuletide festival, which became Christianized as the Twelve Days of Christmas. The setting sun could be very briefly seen shining through the small gap between the capstone of the grand trilithon and the top of one of the sarsens in front of it. In fact it is now in this later stage, the five trilithons that form a horse-shoe shaped circle do come into focus.

In this later phase of Stonehenge the main astronomical events are sighted through the gap between the upright pillars of the trilithons, and not by a line-of-sight formed by the Station Stones. The exception is of course, the summer solstice sunset; this is observed through a trilithon but more specifically from the Altar stone. Also the NE winter moonrise, when occurring in a major standstill, is seen directly from the Altar stone.

So, as diagram 4 shows, the midsummer sunset, occurring in the NW, can now be observed through the Northern trilithon; and the winter moonset, occurring in the NW, in a major standstill, can be seen through the Western trilithon. The winter solstice sunrise is seen through the Eastern trilithon. Whereas the moonrise in the SE, when it occurs at a major standstill, can be seen through the Southern trilithon. One notes here that the moonset in a major standstill in the summer, hence at its most southerly point, is not observable from the trilithon sarsens. And also a minor standstill in the SW is not observable, although some confused reports exist about this, (see last section, Conservative Archaeological Theory).

But what about the eclipses? Could the priests in charge of Stonehenge in its later phases, (Stonehenge III+) predict, and thus prepare for, an eclipse?

We have seen that it allowed an observation of the winter and summer solstice sun set and rise, as well as the extremes of the moon's orbit (the standstills) but what about the really major emphasis on eclipses, which Stonehenge Phase I had? In the early phase of Stonehenge, the 56 Aubrey holes enabled eclipse prediction. It appears indeed that in Stonehenge III stage it was possible to predict eclipses, and indeed the priests could be made very aware of the lunar cycles.

Stonehenge III and the Moon
The assumption has often been made quite naturally that Stonehenge in its later phase was not concerned with the eclipses. But as we noted earlier, when Stonehenge III was created, and the Aubrey holes were no longer in use, an inner horse-shape ring of 19 bluestones were set up in Stonehenge. However, 19 is the number of the lunar nodal cycle (rounded off from 18.6 yrs).

It is very likely that these 19 stones are in fact designed to replace the function of the 56 Aubrey holes; so, these 19 stones were used to predict eclipses. This is a conclusion reached after some brilliant research by an American professor of Astronomy, Sharon Challener, who has discovered how this could be done. An article posted on the web, "Ancients could have used Stonehenge {III} to predict lunar eclipses", by SPACE.com Staff, tells us about this:

> Sharon Challener, a professor of physics and astronomy at Clarion University in Pennsylvania, who has been studying the megalith for more than 20 years, discovered a pattern in the puzzling horseshoe-shaped row of vertical columns at Stonehenge's center. Challener, like so many others, had been trying for years to figure out what was the purpose of Stonehenge. She had speculated about, and tested out, countless celestial cycles as they may have lined up with the mysterious stones.
> Then, almost by accident, she noticed that eclipses are visible from certain locations on Earth in distinct 47

month cycles. That seemed to add up. There were 19 upright columns at the monument's center, which are collectively called the Bluestone Horseshoe. If the Stonehengers placed some stone marker on top of a pillar at one end of the horseshoe during a lunar eclipse and moved the rock to the adjacent pillar every full moon, they could predict successive eclipses.

Moving the rock this way every lunar month, the marker would stand at the center of the horseshoe, after two-and-a-half trips around the row -- 47 months after the original eclipse. The full moon that rose that month would fall into Earth's shadow during the night. That stone could then be taken down and moved to the beginning of the horseshoe again. "It makes use of the youngest, most central, most massive features of Stonehenge and it predicts all lunar eclipses occurring at Stonehenge without predicting a lot of eclipses that wouldn't be visible from the site", Challener said.

No matter how often eclipses are seen within a 47 month cycle, the eclipses that are separated by 47 months are all related to each other. They form a sort of family, she said. A family {of eclipses} begins as a partial, or penumbral eclipse and it recurs every 47 months. Each time it would be a little closer to a total eclipse. There might be a dozen or so total eclipses in the family, and then the eclipses would grow more partial, eclipsing a smaller part of the moon every 47 months until the eclipse failed to appear. That family would then be finished, and the stone that marked it could be retired. (29)

Moreover, as we have noted earlier, there are 30 uprights in the outer circle of sarsens, which are linked together by their lintels or capstones. Now it is also known that a full moon occurs every 29.53 days. But of the 30 stones which make up the outer circle of sarsens, stone 11, which is the southernmost one, is really noticeably smaller. Is it in fact only half the height of the other, only about 2.67 yards (2.44m) above the ground. The others are 13.5 ft tall, making this stone 1.6 yards (1.5m) lower than its neighbour, stone number 10. It is not definitely known whether it has been broken, or whether it was intended to be smaller.

Our conclusion is that it was intentionally made smaller, to represent the 29.5 days of the lunar monthly cycle, and as such it forms part a larger lunar observation feature of Stonehenge, with its 19 bluestones. So, the reconstructions of Stonehenge, which are often very well made, probably should show stone Eleven as much smaller. We remind ourselves here of what we have seen at Stonehenge III as the doorways to celestial events. Its alignments make possible the following:

A: monitoring the lunar nodes standstills
B: the summer solstice sunrise
C: winter solstice sunset, (and sunrise)
D: the predicting of lunar eclipses

At this point, we clearly know the celestial observations that both the earlier and later stages of Stonehenge made possible. But, fascinating though this is, it actually does not answer two fascinating and crucial questions, the "Why?" and the "How?": Why did the Megalithic people wish to do all this and how was it possible to achieve this accuracy? With regard to their reasons, it is clear that knowledge of the seasonal cycle, which allows one to know when it is the summer and winter solstice, and what the Moon is doing, was important to the Neolithic people for agricultural purposes. But, was there another reason for the focus on these astronomical events?

Chapter Five: the astronomical accuracy of ancient sites

Extended consciousness in antiquity?
The question arises concerning a deeper motivation of the Megalithic priests when we consider the sheer amount of effort made to pinpoint the lunar standstills or to predict eclipses. For knowledge of these is not really essential for an agrarian civilisation. Considering the huge amount of work required to achieve this, and the little pragmatic value that these offer, there appears to be some spiritual purpose behind the effort made to experience these events. We noted at the beginning of this section, that its position at 51 degrees north enabled the amazing accuracy of their work, because of the right-angle formed between the lunar node extremes and the solar positions at solstice and equinox, just at this latitude.

At this point we need to note that in fact the awareness itself of the right-angles between these significant phenomena occurring in the sky is not something which the pre-literate Megalithic builders could have achieved by intellectual calculations. The right-angle is created by the angle of inclination of the orbital path of moon to that of the sun. And yet, it is precisely this which was in fact known. How is this possible? Is it coincidence, or did the priests possess some form of psychic capacity, some kind of extended faculty of consciousness, almost unknown today?

As archaeologists quickly point out, Neolithic people could not know of the differing orbital planes of the sun and moon and their complex interaction, just from their observation. The only method of ascertaining this knowledge other than a psychic capacity, requires a civilisation which has developed writing, and has compiled extensive written records. People would have to accumulate an enormous amount of readings of celestial motions, and retain these in written records and consult them over many generations; this is something which, as the archaeologists well know, the Megalithic people did not do. So is it at all possible that the very location of Stonehenge, as well as its complex alignments, were achieved through some kind of psychic consciousness? This may appear at first to be an unlikely theory, but a careful look at ancient cultures shows this idea to be a reasonable theory.

Looking at what we have noted so far, we can summarize the impact of astronomical research into Stonehenge by saying that in effect, astronomers created the new field of scientific research, called archaeo-astronomy. At the amazing ancient Celtic site in Germany, called the Externsteine, the primal Celts created an observatory capable of tracking the so-called lunar node, as well as the summer solstice sunrise. Yet there remains a reluctance to accept these facts about the Externsteine or Stonehenge; archaeo-astronomy is still not universally accepted.

The conclusion that the Neolithic megalithic builders were able to know about the lunar standstill, to identify its location in empty space, and its relation to the sun's orbital path, is simply not acceptable to many archaeologists. Hence, today there are still some archaeologists who reject Hawkins' conclusions (and in Germany not all German archaeologists agree that the remarkable Externsteine site has a similar cosmic alignment). And some of the remarkable alignments or other features of the Great Pyramid remain unacceptable to many Egyptologists. Why is this?

To explore this question even if briefly is crucially important to our quest to understand sacred sites, because we are now actually focusing on a hugely significant theme, namely the use of extended mental skills by earlier humanity, and also by implication, the loss of this in modern times. One could say that in mainstream science, especially in archaeology where real expertise about earlier civilisations is to be found, there is a prejudice against the idea of an holistic consciousness prevailing amongst the Megalithic people, as shown in their sacred sites.

But what does this really mean? The world's foremost archaeologist expert on Stonehenge in earlier decades Prof.

Richard Atkinson, wrote a scathing article of Hawkins epochal book. In a review called "Moonshine over Stonehenge"; he accused Hawkins of being arrogant, slipshod and unconvincing. In fact, there were defects in the map that Hawkins used, and this was seized on by less holistic academics as a basis to reject all of the important discoveries. But later on, after Sir Fred Hoyle's confirmation of Hawkins' work, Atkinson had to retract his statements and agree that there was indeed an astronomical basis to Stonehenge.

So, what was it that so outraged Atkinson? We could also ask, what is it that so irritates Egyptologists when one finds solid evidence of extraordinary technical engineering feats underlying the Great Pyramid? (And we don't mean nonsensical unfounded speculations) For example, such feats as the extreme accuracy in regard to its north-south orientation, or the slight indentation in its huge walls, which, being lined with optically precise polished casing, created a noticeable reflection of light near equinoctial times as the sun rose.

Those archaeologists who know so clearly just how limited earlier humanity was in analytical and technical capacity, and assert that ancient people simply could not do it, do have a valid point. So how could one reconcile a mentality of ancient times, and its very limited technical capacity, with the construction of sacred monuments that have an eerily accurate, precision engineering incorporated in them? Atkinson wrote in effect, that it is simply nonsense to say that the Megalithic people, being a primitive non-literate people, could ever have worked out the mathematics needed to construct a complex and accurate observatory. And on the other side, Prof. Hoyle, upon confirming these astronomical alignments wrote, somewhat bewildered, "that a veritable Newton or Einstein must have been at work". (30)

And here is the core of the mystery: it was impossible for earlier people, **as modern science understands them**, to do this. Yet even so, it was done! So, Atkinson and his colleagues are correct in disbelieving; yet, since it was done, Atkinson's conclusion is wrong. Likewise, Prof. Hoyle and all those who confirm such amazing alignments and engineering feats are correct, but if they think it was "done by an Einstein", they are wrong, too! The Megalithic people did construct sites with the ability to track subtle and complex astronomical motions, but they did it as primitive people, emerging from the Stone Age. How can such contradictory truths be possible?

The changing mindset of humanity over the millennia
The way to solve this enigma lies in a theory that could be called historical sociology. The theory that says there has been an evolution of consciousness; and people in earlier epochs of time were very different from modern humanity, as regards their consciousness. This theory postulates that people were inwardly different to us both in terms of the inner sensing of their own self, or personal consciousness, and also in terms of how much of the spectrum of reality they had access to. In other words, life in earlier times gave people a different sort of consciousness to what we have today.

Their perception of the environment may have been different to ours, they may have had an extended field of perception; seeing or at least sensing energies that we no longer perceive. This view does not deny the tendency towards superstitiousness amongst pre-literate people; it simply suggests that there was present also an extended perception, a sensing of non-material things. Perhaps they could see and detect subtle energies which modern humanity can no longer detect. It appears to be the case that the Megalithic people (and other ancient peoples) had extended consciousness faculties that have now disappeared.

In any event, it is quite clear in literature from earlier millennia that the spirit beings referred in fairy folklore or myths, etc, were considered by earlier humanity to be objective realities. They believed they saw these things, through a psychic ability. Was it on the basis of enhanced powers of sight that the priests of the Megalithic people could accurately perceive such subtle cosmic processes as the nodal extremes of the Moon's orbit? As we approach modern times the previous psychic consciousness fades, and awareness that earlier peoples once possessed such an extended mental capacity, is forgotten.[13]

So a modern humanistic scientist, like Prof. Atkinson, quite unaware of this change in human consciousness, would naturally be deeply perplexed at the idea of the ancient Egyptians or the Megalithic people, with very little aptitude for sophisticated technology, building a temple which is oriented with a precision that only 20th century science could equal, and only if the engineers used sophisticated instruments. As Hawkins pointed out in his book *Stonehenge Decoded*, the huge trilithons of Stonehenge are accurately sited to within four inches, and if they were less accurately placed than this, they would not have had the precision needed to create the openings out to the celestial event.

Now, to really feel what Stonehenge is about, one has to ask if these people had a type of extended, holistic consciousness how would the extremes of the moon's motions be inwardly experienced by them? Today, we still find a full moon rising up somewhere out in nature has a lovely ambience, but what if we had the extended perceptual ability of a priest in antiquity? How would these extreme lunar motions, and also the eclipses, be experienced? To find the answer, we need to briefly explore the consciousness of people who lived long ago, when Stonehenge was being constructed.

That temples were built with an astronomical alignment, or indeed that many burial sites were constructed with a celestial alignment, reveals something very important, something that has become clearer in recent sociological studies. Namely that

---

[13] The general concept of consciousness evolving is found in mainstream sociological studies, and the additional nuance of going from psychic and group oriented to more individuated and non-psychic is found in western esoteric literature, e.g., the works of Rudolf Steiner (1861-1925)

the ancients, with their different mind-set, experienced the solar system on another level of existence. To these people, it had a spiritual quality. To them, a full moon or an eclipse, the zodiac constellations, or the summer and winter solstices, were not just events of practical importance for their agricultural society; they had a personal significance, with a sacred or religious overtone. Such was the significance, in the earlier ages, of this extended perception, and such was the prestige of the priests who manifested this, that such vast projects as the Great Pyramid and Stonehenge were undertaken. It is useful at this point to review the celestial alignments of Stonehenge:

What was seen through the lines-of-sight?

From Stonehenge I & II:
A: two lunar major Standstills (at most northern moonset, most southern moonrise)
B: the summer solstice sunrise
C: winter solstice sunset, (and sunrise)
D: a detailed predicting of either lunar or solar eclipses

From Stonehenge III:
A: three lunar major Standstills
B: the summer solstice sunrise
C: winter solstice sunset, (and sunrise)
D: the predicting of lunar eclipses

The lunar standstills that Stonehenge was aligned to were those that occurred at the moonrise in winter and summer, and at the moonset in wintertime. We can see that in Stonehenge Stage III, there was more focus on lunar events, but as we shall consider below, in this later phase there was still a strong solar focus. To find out what that was, we need to understand more about why they wanted to have lines-of-sight to various events such the eclipses, and especially why they wanted the large shadow-fields as well. For, as we shall see, large shadowed areas have been especially designed to be part of Stonehenge.

Why monitor eclipses?
If we conclude that earlier humanity, including the Megalithic people, had some kind of extended consciousness or enhanced sensitivity to nature, we can explore the question, what was the religious purpose of Stonehenge? We know **what** it actually allowed people to observe, but **why** did they want to observe this? For example, why would a lunar major standstill be of interest to the Megalithic people, to people with some form of holistic sensing?

Well, when a major standstill occurs, as we have noted, there is a corresponding major change in the way the moon is seen to move across the sky. The moon will be seen in the northern hemisphere coming up over the horizon much further to the north (this means becoming much more prominent), and then rising up higher in the sky, much nearer to the zenith or overhead point) than the sun would, even if it were the summertime.

But only two weeks later, the moon will be seen coming up over the horizon much further to the south, and then only rising up very low in the sky. It moves across the sky even lower than sun would go if it were the cold winter days. But all of this is only a description of the visual change. If we think about this unusual phenomenon, we can start to sense how the moon at these special times when it rose so high, must have induced a really potent ambience in the atmosphere, to the subtle sensing of the Megalithic people and their priests.

Even for modern matter-of-fact people, a full moon has a special ambience, how much more so would this have been, if one could detect (or believed one could detect) subtle lunar energies. It is well known today that people who have various pathological states of mind, and those who have a more psychic mind-set, are potently affected by the full moon. Perhaps the *intensity* of these experiences (not their disturbed quality) give us an idea of just how much impact the full moon made to our ancestors. And this situation applied even more strongly in a major standstill when the moon rose up so very high. Then two weeks later the moon moved off to the south, and stayed very low above the horizon. This time of greatly reduced lunar energies would have been another very strange time to people with a naturally enhanced sensitivity.

A lunar eclipse occurs when the moon, which of course shines from the reflected light of the sun, becomes dark because the Earth has moved between the moon and the sun. In modern times we just find it mildly interesting and we gather to look at it. But to the ancients this was a sinister time, a time when wholesome celestial processes are interrupted, and malignant energies intensify. Folklore about eclipses from many peoples of earlier times testifies to this.

So we can conclude that monitoring of the lunar standstills would have been a vital part of the spiritual tasks of the early priests. Perhaps to the Megalithic people, the lunar eclipse would have been rather like a reversed Jacob's ladder. Jacob's ladder is mentioned in the Bible (Genesis 28:12), when it describes how Jacob during a spiritual experience saw a vision of divine spiritual beings ascending upwards, from the sky into celestial realms. A lunar eclipse is presented in older folklore as a time when malignant beings descended down to the Earth.

Stonehenge in its early stages could also predict solar eclipses, and these, like lunar eclipses, were also regarded as a time when sinister energies were prowling around. In a solar eclipse the moon moves in between the sun and the Earth, blocking the sunlight from shining down upon the Earth, and thus casting its shadow down onto the Earth.

A study of the attitudes of earlier peoples reveals that the belief existed across far-flung parts of the world that, during an eclipse something malignant is activated in the heavens, and this something may descend into the community. So it was the custom to protect the household from these descending malignant energies. People would turn their pots and pans upside down to stop bad influences entering them; crops would not be harvested, seeds were not sown, and so on. An eclipse was regarded as a time when unwholesome energies appear, affecting the Earth through the funnel of darkness which the eclipse creates. (31)

In fact it was also the case in Mesopotamia amongst the ancient Babylonians at the same time as Stonehenge was being developed, that a lunar eclipse was an omen of extreme evil. In texts known as Enuma-Anu-Enlil, which go back to about 1950 BC, it is stated that during a lunar eclipse, under certain circumstances, the king might die (from the release of malignant energies). Consequently, if an ill-omened eclipse looked imminent, a duplicate king would be put on the throne, and once the eclipse was over he was usually killed, (if he had not died already from the sinister eclipse, of course!).

From the foreknowledge of an eclipse predicted by the priests at Stonehenge, word would have been spread around and the people would have been alerted to protect themselves in this regard. We modern people may still feel that an eclipse is only a physical phenomenon, affecting just the flow of sunlight to the earth, and anything thing else is mere superstition. But is this because, without knowing it, we are now equipped with only a limited capacity for perception?

There is now scientific interest in a phenomenon called the Saros cycle that occurs every 18 years, and is connected to the times when eclipses can occur. Scientists have discovered that subtle energies flowing through our planet's atmosphere are affected by this lunar eclipse cycle. In particular, they have noted that at an eclipse, some energy affects the incomplete (isotopic) form of carbon, known as carbon 14. This is a partly energy, partly material, form of carbon; in effect it is ethereal carbon.

The record of its activity in the atmosphere is enshrined inside trees, in the annual rings made as it grows. And it is clear that something is causing a disturbance, a variation to the normal state of this subtle energy particle, as it pulses through the atmosphere. Scientific research has concluded that as a Saros cycle occurs, (that is an alignment of sun, earth and moon which could cause an eclipse), a definite change occurs in the subtle energetic particles in the Earth's upper atmosphere. This change lasts for one hour, in each 18-year cycle. This is due to a change in the energies existing inside the shadow of the anti-solar side of the moon. The shadow sweeps through the upper atmosphere, and produces a tangible effect on the Earth, which can be detected in the ring patterns inside the trunks of trees. See the Appendix for a fuller description of this.

Now, the priests at Stonehenge in both its early and late stages could of course determine the summer solstice day by observing the sun rising very close to the Heel Stone. To know the peak of the sun's path is crucial to determining the seasonal cycle, and this is important for agricultural purposes. Stonehenge in both its stages was also able to provide a line-of-sight to the winter solstice sunset, which is the shortest day and the longest night of the year. To determine this day is also a vital part of keeping track of the seasons. But, there was probably also a spiritual reason for this.

For example, with the Celtic people of the British Isles, the third day after the winter solstice sunset signalled the beginning of the 12 day period of Yuletide, or the time of the Holy Nights; the holiest time in the Celtic calendar. For ages there had been a tradition of solemnly refraining from both work and play, to mark this festival period.

It was not until the 1930's that this tradition faded out in outlying Scottish islands. (32) The focus then was on the spiritual theme of 'light in the darkness', a theme that is still present in the Christian festival of the midwinter Christmas; which in Britain and Europe was a 12-day event.

But very importantly the stones that allowed these lines-of-sight are also really huge. So the question can be asked, are they blocking out something? What caused the Megalithic people to use such huge stones? Because, these alignments or lines-of-sight could have been set up quite easily without using 40 ton stones; simple wooden poles would have been quite satisfactory. Knowing about the old holistic consciousness of earlier times, we can now examine the alignments of Stonehenge, and discover why these alignments are there, and why so many huge shadow-fields are there, too.

Chapter Six: Another secret of Stonehenge: shadow-fields

Deliberately creating shadow-fields

At this point we need to briefly note the unconvincing arguments of some non-holistic academic people about the purpose of Stonehenge. John North's book, *Stonehenge, Neolithic Man and the Cosmos*, is the largest and most detailed of these writings, and yet it is disappointing for those seeking insight into Stonehenge. (33) He is not an archaeologist; his specialty is the history of the Exact Sciences. Although he provides really useful data for archaeology, showing that Neolithic tombs are often aligned to a star or a solar position, his conclusions about Stonehenge are disappointing in their narrowness.

For his conclusion is that Stonehenge is oriented to the SW (where the sun sets in winter), not to the NE where the sun rises in summer, and that therefore the amazing alignments of the stone circles are of minimal significance in Stonehenge (!). Indeed he concludes that people stood outside the sarsens, near the Heel Stone to experience what Stonehenge has to offer.

He emphasizes that if at sunset on the winter solstice, one gazed back at the centre of the sarsen circle, from out at the Heel Stone, then a small gap was to be seen in the furthest away circle of stones, between the horizontal capstones of the smaller uprights and raised slightly above these the largest trilithon, the Grand Trilithon. In this gap one could see the last rays of the setting sun. He then also adds that another line-of-sight was also there, with a focus on the setting moon.

His thesis is examined briefly in the Appendix. Fortunately, the core of his argument for believing that there was a SW focus has been very effectively proven to be fully in error. This was done, ironically enough, by a conservative archaeologist, L. Sims, who replaced it with an even less convincing argument. (We shall briefly examine their ideas at the end of this chapter).

However John North does point out that long ago, when Stonehenge was viewed from the direction of the rising sun (the East, and NE), before it was partially dismantled or damaged, the monument would appear to the viewer **as if made of a solid wall of stone**. He points out that the builders,

> "…achieved this by adjusting the ratio of the width of the stones to the gap between them and by nesting the horseshoe arrangement of five trilithons within the sarsen circle. This design allowed the trilithons to block nearly all the gaps that otherwise would be seen through the sarsen ring."

Now, unknown to J. North, and to Stonehenge researchers in general, it is this aspect of the monument which gives us a hint to discovering a major purpose of Stonehenge. This secret concerns the role that shadows played in the construction and design of Stonehenge. To provide some orientation in this idea of the shadow-fields, it's helpful to briefly look at other sacred sites of the Megalithic people, such as those of Carnac and Cornwall.

Strange capped chambers in Carnac and Cornwall
We have considered some prominent Megalithic monuments, in order to get some orientation in regard to important sacred sites of the Megalithic people of Britain and Western Europe. We have seen that some of the more sophisticated monuments have subterranean chambers, and also often an astronomical orientation. We have concluded that these, if they have no sign of being used as tomb (or were used for this only in a later phase) then they were very likely to have been used for some form of religious activity. However there is another type of sacred monument from the Megalithic people that we really need to look at now: the capped chambers. That is, a simple enclosure made of large slabs of rock, which has a horizontal slab placed on top, capping the structure.

Now, when reading about these you will see that they are catalogued together with subterranean tombs. In other words they are regarded as a form of tomb, even though they are (mainly) above the ground. It is important to note that the Megalithic people had been building underground tombs since ca. 4,500 BC. So, we don't wish to deny that quite substantial graves, in the form of underground chambers, were constructed by these people. But there are also these strangely simple, capped chambers that are empty, and show no signs of ever being used for burials; they just don't have a grave-like quality.

One place where many burial chambers (cairns or earthen mounds) and many capped chambers are to be found (above ground or just a little underground), apart from the British Isles, is in France, in Brittany. Many of these monuments are referred to as "corridor dolmens", and they are all classified as tombs. Many of them may well be just that.

There are some larger ones that have decorations and even a form of altar in them, so it is clear that some form of ceremony took place in these tombs. In these chambers small numbers of people gathered to perform religious rites for the souls of the dead, just as happened in the impressive mortuary temples and tombs on the Giza plateau of Egypt.

But are all of these capped chambers in Britain and Ireland and in France really just graves? Look at some chambers in England, existing on open moorland in Cornwall. These chambers show every sign of being shadow-chambers, and not tombs; the Trethevey chamber or quoit as it is locally known, is shown in illustration 5. It consists of a large capstone, looking like a gigantic table top, held up by a few upright stones.

A fine old drawing of this monument, made about 200 years ago by an antiquarian, does show in a striking way a quality that these have; they create a shadow-field. The images in illustration 5 of the Trethevy and the Lanyon quoits show how

66

these monuments, rising high up above the flat moorland, were too tall to be used as some kind of Druidic altar, and far too open to ever be a used as a tomb.

There are quite a number of these, but many have collapsed over the millennia. It also has to be said that some of these collapsed ruins were probably tombs, and were (or still are) covered extensively with soil and small rocks. But some of them are not tombs; they are something else. See illustrations 5 and 6 and ask yourself, are these really tombs; would the Megalithic people place their dead in such an exposed structure? Why place the deceased in a covered-over chamber? Why did they not simply dig a simple grave? Or if it is a tomb built above the ground, then surely the builders would construct a properly sealed-off cairn at least, one which is no longer open to the air.

Mainstream archaeological theory replies that the soil which once covered the bare cairn somehow dissipated. But it has long been noted that the conclusion that all such rock chambers were burial sites, from which the soil has dissipated over time, is a dubious idea. As R. MacAlister, Professor of Celtic Archaeology wrote, back in 1920,

> It is impossible to explain what has happened to the earth {the covering soil} if we are to suppose that the dolmens were always covered in. Moreover in many cases, such as the fine dolmen at Legananny, Co. Down (Ireland), the supporting stones {for the capstone} are so far apart that they would not hold back the earth from running in, under the capstone, and {thereby} filling-in the chamber which the uprights were presumably intended to make. (34) In Brittany, especially at Carnac, in addition to burial sites there are the world-famous long rows of menhirs, or standing stones, which obviously have a spiritual meaning,   and   are   not   tombs.

5   Cornwall Shadow-chambers
Used by the Druids for research into seasonal influences

Above: the Lanyon quoit
Below: A fine line drawing from long ago of the Trethevy quoit

68

6   Carnac shadow-chambers
Top: the shadow-chamber at Crucuno near Carnac
Bottom: the shadow-chamber at Mane-Kerioned near Carnac

So it is possible that the Megalithic people also did construct some monuments designed for religious rites at such a remarkable site, and not only tombs. Especially these open-air rock chambers that appear never to have been closed-off with soil, appear to have a different purpose.

And indeed just this possibility is even allowed in mainstream archaeology with regard to some Megalithic monuments in the Carnac area. It is said that certain capped monuments may have a strange purpose. These monuments aren't normally accessed by tourists. According to an official guide to the famous Carnac region of France, there are a number of such "enigmatic" underground Celtic sites in the region around Carnac. For example,

> "The Mané Roullarde passage grave on the north side of La Trinité-Sur-Mer is in very bad condition. Nearby, the Gauls have built some stranger, enigmatic subterranean passages, capped with {stone} slabs." (35)

So here we have it: these are a form of chamber somewhat underground with capstones, chambers that are not actually classified as tombs. They are still today unclassified because they are an enigma. Unfortunately, these aren't a priority item to the antiquity authorities in this region of France, so they have yet to be properly explored, so no pictures or descriptions of these monuments have been made available so far. Illustration 6 shows these quoits.

So not only in Cornwall but in Brittany too, amidst the many grave-sites there are some monuments above the ground, which although classified as tombs, actually appear to be something else. These are strange chambers that are capped with large stones that just don't have a tomb-like quality. These rock chambers in Carnac made with very thick slabs of stone obviously form an enclosure; and yet they were not tombs.

Some of these show no signs of ever being a tomb. Indeed some are referred to in archaeological literature simply as chambers.

We maintain that this is exactly what they were: shadow-chambers. Some of these intriguing chambers, built on a slight mound, may have an actual grave incorporated near it, a few yards from these other spaces. So these spaces are not graves, but they are chambers that cover the person inside, they make a place where one can be hidden away from the sunlight, in the shadows.

But looking at the Lanyon quoit for example, it does suggest that the priests of the Megalithic people sat inside them, in order to observe something. It is our conclusion that these chambers were a form of observation chamber, in which the sunlight is halted by the thick rock. But if the sunlight were halted, what would penetrate through the rock? As modern science is well aware, there are many other energies in the atmosphere, none of which are visible to our eyes, such as ultra-violet light, infra-red, gamma rays, x-rays, etc. But the fact that they are invisible to us does not mean that they do not exist. Biologists are aware that some animals can see some of these energies; for example there are birds that can see the ultra-violet rays.

It is then an intriguing suggestion that the priests of the Megalithic people with their extended perceptual capacities, found it was much easier to observe subtle influences raying in from the atmosphere at key seasonal times, from within their shadow-chambers.[14] Modern radio-astronomy has been slowly discovering ever more remarkable and previously unsuspected energies that bathe our planet continually. Did the Megalithic people see some of these? The British Celtic priests were regarded as seers, and no doubt the earlier Megalithic priests as well, so it is not out of the question that these people had developed some form of higher perception.

---

[14] This radical new idea was first suggested by the famous Goethe scholar, Rudolf Steiner, in 1920 during a visit to England.

Early Stonehenge (stages I & II) and its shadow-fields

Let's now consider Stonehenge from the viewpoint of its shadow-fields. The archaeologist L. Sims writing about Stonehenge supports the deeply unconvincing argument that it had its main alignment on the winter solstice. (36) He suggests, as does the historian of exact science, J. North, that the sarsens were in effect unimportant, and that in order to witness the winter sunset people actually gathered on the grand Avenue that led off from the stone circle, past the Heel Stone to the Northeast, rather than inside the stone circles.

But Sims also comments that at the midsummer sunrise, when people looked to the rising sun, they again stayed out of the irrelevant stone circles, and instead again gathered on the Avenue. Sims comments that if they were inside the stone circles, then their view of the rising sun **would be badly obscured by the stones themselves** and by any trees outside. Sims writes that it would be illogical if people set out to celebrate the midsummer sunrise from inside Stonehenge! For that would mean to celebrate this event, they gathered before dawn on the Grand Avenue where the Heel Stone is situated, and walked up to the stone circles and entered into the stone circle enclosure, and then, very awkwardly turned around, trying to gaze back at the midsummer sun. He writes that this would be strange,

> ....it would be a very odd ritual centre indeed if, once having turned their backs {on the rising sun} and walked away from the rising sun along the Avenue and into the monument, participants were then expected to turn around {to face the sun}, ignore the monument, face back towards the rising summer solstice sun, and observe it {rising up} outside the monument {where it was} probably emerging from ....obstacles, {like the stone sarsens, and any trees outside the circle}
> (clarifying comments in brackets from this author)

In other words, it would be much more sensible to simply stay standing on the Avenue, to get a good view of the rising sun.

Now this is a very significant criticism! Here we can recall the comment from John North, that Stonehenge would have looked like a solid wall made of rock uprights, when viewed from the Heel Stone, which is quite some yards to the NE of the monument. Its stone circles would indeed block the sun. The value of these two comments is that they actually point us in the right direction, to discover another fascinating secret of Stonehenge.

It was designed not only to allow amazingly accurate celestial observation, but also to cast substantial shadows, **to create what we can call shadow-fields.** Because indeed it truly would be a self-defeating exercise to walk up into the stone circles and then try to look at the rising sun, now obscured by all those stone uprights.

A good place to begin looking at the role of shadows in Stonehenge is with the Heel Stone. It stands inside its own ditch at the Northeast entrance from the Avenue. Sims presents the most potent argument against the Heel Stone, as a marker for the midsummer sunrise:

> .....standing at the centre of the sarsen circle, and looking through either eye, the summer solstice sun does not rise over the Heel Stone. It did not in the Neolithic Age and it never has. The sun has always risen by about three solar diameters (about 1.5°) to the left of the Heel Stone. Since other monuments of the period had higher levels of accuracy in their alignments, this is an unacceptable level of error for one of the greatest of these monuments (North 1996; Ruggles 1999a).

Now Sims is right that the sun rises on the summer solstice slightly to the left of the stone; and this had led to the theory that perhaps it once was one of a pair of stones. These two stones together would have created a defined line-of-sight in which the sun would then appear. However, this is not proof that the builders made huge errors in their calculations.

For, this siting of the stones is really accurate, and the other astronomical alignments are proof enough of the capacity of the builders of Stonehenge to be very precise. The placement of the Heel Stone allows one to track its motion upwards, as it climbs slowly up to the NE; and that was probably a specific need of the priests. But here we need to realize that Stonehenge is very much about the creating of shadows. For, just by being precisely just to the left, the rising sun **would cast its substantial shadow straight into the central sarsens**. At this time its shadow is 120 yards (110m) in length, reaching right up to the stone circle.

And now, a very significant fact: the Heel Stone is not a heel stone at all. It has nothing to do with a heel. That term comes from some much older era; this stone is in fact referred to in older English literature as the hele stone. The term hele goes back to Old English, when it was not hele but helan. **The term helan means to conceal or hide or cover**. And from helan there came another word, heolstor, which means darkness or cover, or hiding place. (37) So, the heel Stone was actually the Helan Stone, or **the Covering Stone or the Hiding Stone**!

This is very significant when considered with a feeling for the holistic attitude of ancient peoples, for it holds the key to understanding why this stone, and the sarsen circles, were erected in the way they were. It is not called the heel stone, but the Cover-Stone that is, the shadow-making Stone, because it conceals or covers up the sunlight, **by making shadows**. Its purpose was to cast a shadow, as well as to be a general guide as to the sun's motions!

At this point we should note the research of scholars in the 19th century into the terms used for such stone monuments, by people in areas around Megalithic sites. They found that a prominent term for them in the UK, in France and in Germany was "the sun-stones", and "sun-circles". See illustration 7 which shows how the Cover Stone and the four Station Stones of Stonehenge I & II would have acted as shadow-fields.

So, here we are not looking at the lines-of-sight (which are also important), but the shadow-fields blocking the sunlight, which the same markers also created. So the focus on the sun, or rather the spiritual influences of the sun, which was a focus in Egyptian monuments, and also at the Externsteine with its midsummer sunrise chamber, is also happening at Stonehenge. But in contrast to the ancient Egyptian culture, with the Megalithic priests the sunlight was observed from within the shadows cast by the great circle of sarsens, and by the Cover Stone. Subtle energies within the sunlight were observed in the shadows which blocked out the bright sunlight.

Later Stonehenge (stage III +) and its shadow-fields
Now when the sophisticated sarsens were set up, with their capstones and the bluestones circles, and the five large Trilithons, then the classic Stonehenge that we know today came about. As we have shown, these were oriented to specific lines-of-sight. But also all these stone uprights had another purpose: they were creating many large shadow-fields. Every drawing of Stonehenge has to show, if it is realistic, many extensive shadows.

There must be a reason for the extensive use of huge stone slabs: we conclude that it was to create areas of shadow in which the sunlight was blocked off. Did the Druids, like the priests at Carnac and Cornwall, position themselves in these shadow fields in order to contemplate what their extended vision revealed to them in the shadows cast on Midsummer's Day?

See illustration 8, this shows the very substantial extent of the shadow-fields created by the action of the stones, blocking the sun's rays, on the summer solstice. In any event, Sims is right, in a sense: no-one would walk up inside the wonderful sarsen circle and turn around to observe the sunrise, only to find the rising sun substantially blocked by the sarsens themselves, and the trees, etc.

7 Stonehenge I & II: shadow-areas

The shadows cast at sun rise on the **summer solstice by the Heel Stone**. It is not a 'Heel' stone, it is in old English the 'Helan Stone. Helan means 'cover/conceal'. This stone covers up (blocks) the sunlight; so it is the Shadow Stone or Cover Stone.

Monitored the shadows cast by the **four Station Stones** on the **summer solstice**, and at sunrise and also at sunset on the winter solstice, known later as the 12 day Yuletide. These shadows would also have been experienced in the simple wooden temple-like building. The predicting of eclipses and determining of lunar nodes [standstill] are also happening here, but not relevant to the shadow-capability.

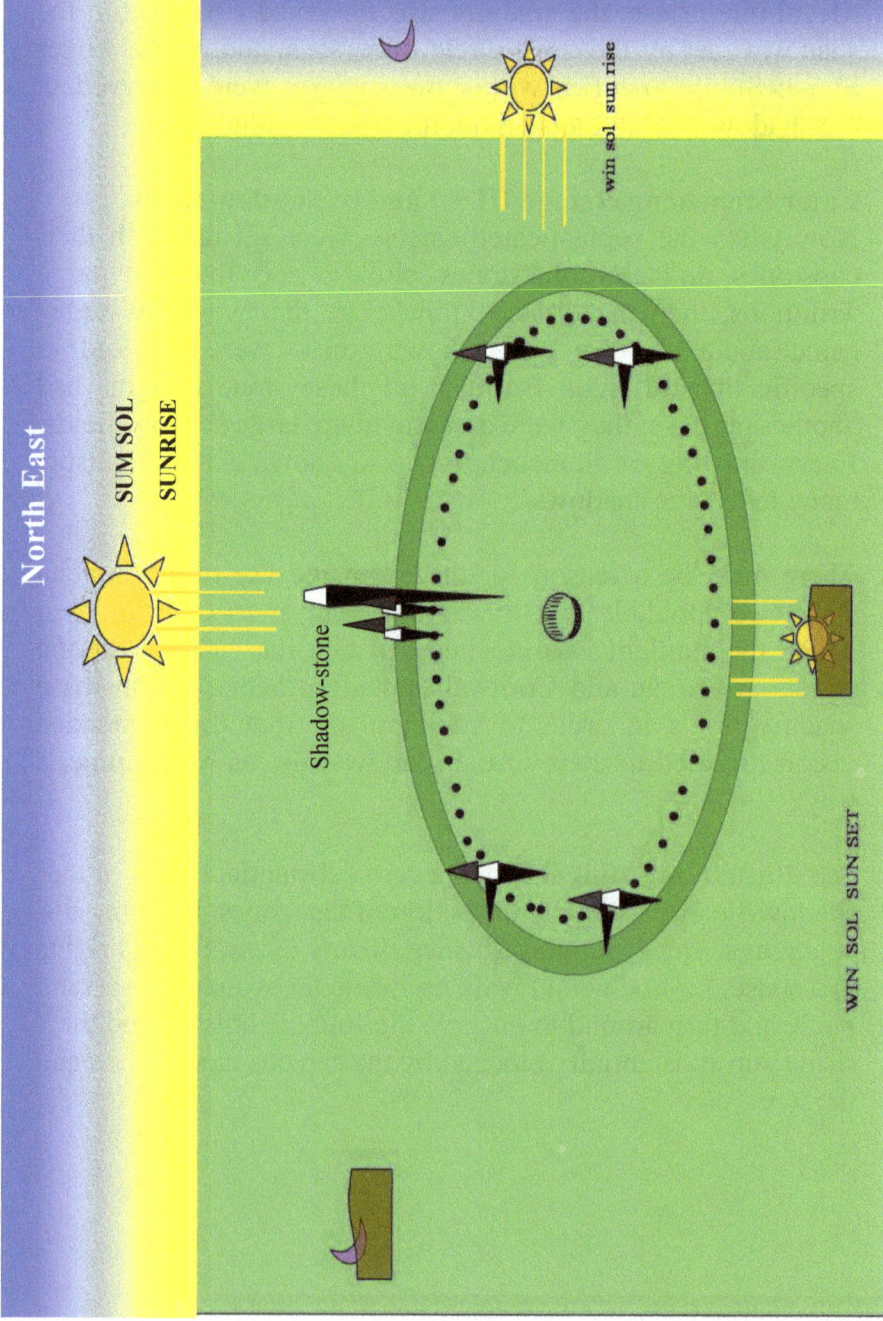

North East

SUM SOL SUNRISE

Shadow-stone

win sol sun rise

WIN SOL SUN SET

It is very likely that the Druids never wanted to watch the sunrise from inside the sacred circle, because of the obstacles made by the huge stone uprights. So, were they there, inside the Stonehenge sarsen circle to spiritually observe, from inside a shadow-field not the obscured sun, but the star influences which were in-streaming during midsummer's day? Energies which the priests felt were difficult to see in the glare of the sunlight. If so, then they were no doubt also positioned for this purpose in the very long shadow-field cast by the Cover Stone.

And so North's point, that the stone circle would have looked like a solid wall of rock now takes on its correct significance; what does a solid wall of rock cause, when the Sun is rising? It creates a dense shadow-field! This indicates that the builders formed the stone circles of Stonehenge in such a way as to create an extensive shadow effect.

Stonehenge as a shadow-field observatory
In essence, it is our conclusion that apart from actual tombs some of these megalithic chambers especially the huge sarsen formations of Stonehenge, created in fact a shadow-filled space for the priest to undertake what they viewed as serious research into the subtle qualities of the prevailing atmospheric energies. So, just as the Shadow Stone blocked the sunlight, by making a shadow-field, so too, the sarsen circles concealed the sunlight, and thereby made shadow-fields.

If you have ever tried to see subtle atmospheric phenomena, you will also, in researching these, avoid staring into the bright glare of the sunlight. For example, those faint slanting lines of darkness which appear in bright sunny days, and are not caused by little clouds creating impediments to the rays of light, (best seen when gazing out over a hilltop or over the ocean), or those enigmatic little darting points of light which at times fill the dusk or dawn sky.

The stone circles: Note the shadows, not the lines of sight; the sarsens deliberately create extensive shadow-areas

The Helan Stone: the shadow it casts on the summer solstice sunrise reaches to the sarsens.

The Shadow Stone

8 The Shadows of Stonehenge III

The Altar Stone may have been lying flat, and not upright

The shadows cast by the tall, thick stone uprights are very extensive, and effectively hold back the glare of the sun (the visible–light rays), but not other rays

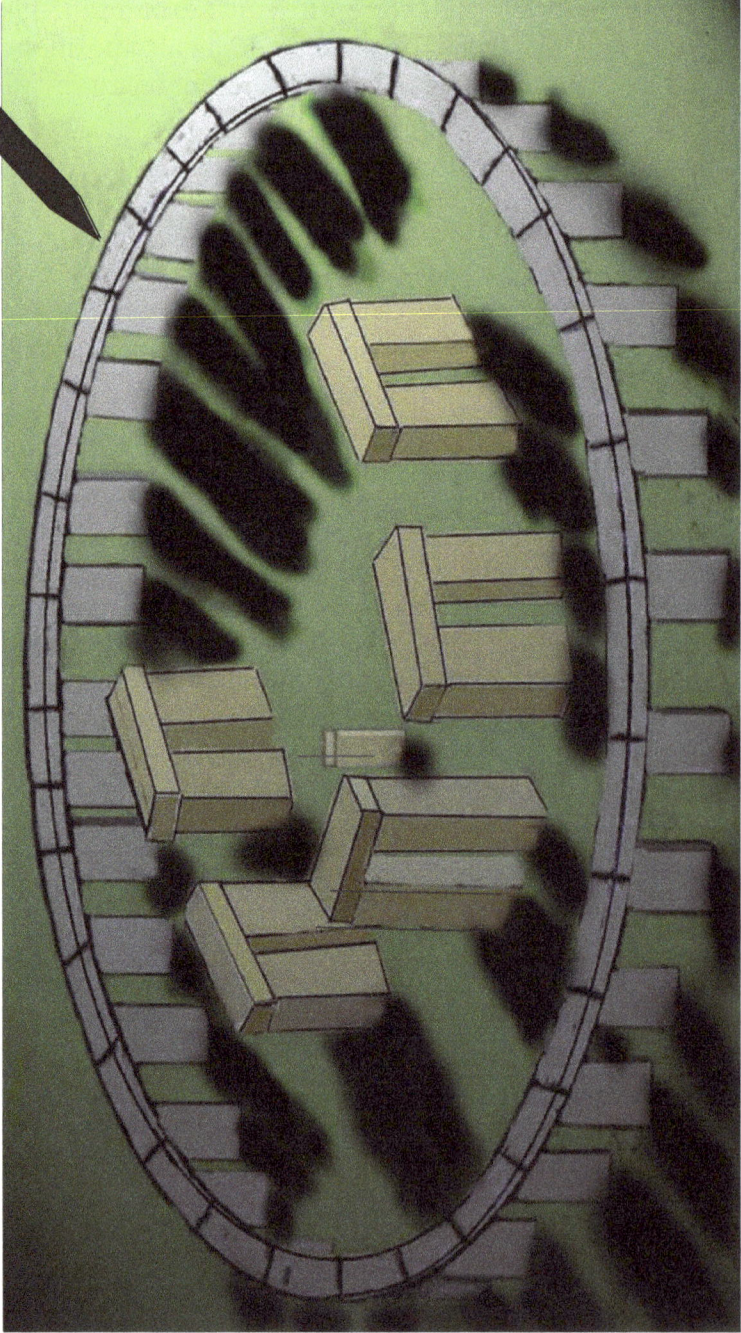

If the observing priest was exposed to the bright glare of the sunlight, then these subtle energies could not be seen, they would be whited-out, and thus not perceptible. So, as the sun rose up and the shadows were cast by the great stones, did the priests focus their attention on the mix of subtle terrestrial energies, or cosmic influences were present in the atmosphere, and how they were changed by the lunar phases?

Although there are no written records from the Megalithic people on this theme or another subject, we do have very substantial evidence of their focus on the stars and planets, from the deliberate orientation of their tombs. The priests of the Megalithic peoples may have sought to research such energies as they manifested behind the sunlight during the daytime. Now, for us today this idea of shadow-chambers is at first startling, but no other theory really accounts for the primitive shadow-chambers of Brittany and Cornwall and for the large shadow-fields of Stonehenge.

The old Celtic fairy lore and weather-folklore of Brittany and the UK, with its reference to strange energies and stranger nature-beings, is an echo of the beliefs and spirituality of the older Megalithic religion. So we may assume that for the Megalithic people, the observation chambers were a way to observe such non-physical things. This could include zodiacal phenomena as well.

It was this interest in celestial alignments that archaeologists set out to understand, after the severe challenge which Hawkins' work caused for them in the 20th century. The earlier nineteenth century research that had already begun to discover the alignments of Stonehenge had been sidelined. But the new research consequently discovered that hundreds of tombs in the British Isles are oriented towards the rising of a planet or a prominent star.

So, the celestial bodies (and their energies) were definitely of great interest to the Megalithic people. Indeed, since many of the stone circles set up by the Megalithic people have twelve upright stone rocks, and were oriented to specific seasonal times of the sun rising, it is quite possible that the priests of the Megalithic people, like their colleagues in Mesopotamia and Egypt, were also seeking to discern zodiac energies But not in the night-time, rather in the day time as they rayed-in and intermingled with solar energies.

Chapter Seven: links between Stonehenge and ancient Greece?

The Greek connection

Before we finish our exploration of Stonehenge it's important to note some evidence which suggests that this colossal achievement did not exist in isolation from other nations. News of this extraordinary sacred site, with its complex astronomical alignments may have spread far beyond the shores of Britain. It appears quite possible that Stonehenge was known to the ancient Greeks, and to pre-Grecian civilisations such as Mycenae.

Such a connection seems to be confirmed by some intriguing archaeological discoveries in grave-sites around Stonehenge. Precious artefacts of great value, both religious and monetary, made of bronze, gold or amber have been discovered in barrow graves on the Wiltshire Plains, near Stonehenge. Professor Piggott who made these discoveries, concluded after careful assessment of the artefacts that these were from ancient Mycenae and Knossos. Professor Richard Atkinson also concluded that a connection to Mycenae exists.

All sorts of theories have arisen from this conclusion; including whether Stonehenge itself was constructed under the supervision of Mycenaean priests, etc. The theme remains disputed and challenging to this day. More recent archaeological views see the such discoveries as evidence of trade between the ancient Aegean cultures and Britain. Or that the objects are only accidentally similar to those of the ancient Grecian world, or were made in Brittany. But there is some interesting evidence in the artefacts and in ancient Greek records which suggests that perhaps the current view is not seeing the full significance of these discoveries.

The most astonishing artefact found is a ritual dagger of the highest imaginable technical skill. It is a dagger that has embedded in its wooden handle some 140,000 rivets of pure gold, each rivet is as fine as a human hair, and each was placed in individually drilled minute holes! But before we examine the archaeological evidence, let's check out the historical records and legends about the communication between the ancient pre-Grecian cultures around the Aegean Sea and Stonehenge.

The Greeks of course knew the British Isles. In about 500 BC Hecateus, son of Hegesander of Miletus, wrote a description of Britain, from the viewpoint of a sea-faring map-maker. And in approximately 300 BC Pytheas of Massilia sailed around Britain, and no doubt went on shore and explored, to a limited extent. Researchers have noted a striking passage in the writings of Sicilian historian Diodorus Siculus, written about 50 BC, in which he describes a temple in the land of the Hyperboreans.

This name is of uncertain meaning, but it does imply people who live some distance from Greece to the north, in a general way. Much discussion exists as to just who these Hyperboreans were. Some ancient Greek texts relate this location to the people living around the lower Danube River area. But some scholars have concluded that it refers to the British Isles, for good reasons. For example, the habitation of these people is quite specifically described as an island, and not just an area around a river on the Continent.

It appears reasonable to conclude that these people can be identified as the people of Britain. Diodorus Siculus refers to older records, partly historical, partly legendary, about the land of the Hyperboreans. These records say this island has a great spherical temple, in the vicinity of a large festive town. This may well be Stonehenge, and Durrington Walls,

> … Hecateus and certain others say that in the region beyond the land of the Celts (Gaul) there lies in the {Atlantic} ocean, an island no smaller than Sicily. This island… is inhabited by the Hyperboreans… there is also on the island a magnificent sacred precinct of Apollo and a notable temple adorned with many votive

offerings, and spherical in shape. A city is there which is sacred to this god...They also say how the moon viewed from this island appears to be but a little distance from the earth... the god visits the island every 19 years, the period in which the return of the stars to the same place in the heavens is accomplished; and for this reason the 19-year period is called by the Greeks the year of Meton. At the time of this appearance of the god {Apollo}, he both plays on the cithara and dances continuously the night ....

The Hyperboreans also have a language which, we are informed {in an ancient legendary account}, is peculiar to themselves, and they are most friendly disposed towards the Greeks, and especially towards the Athenians and Delians, who have inherited this goodwill from most ancient times. This same myth also relates that certain Greeks visited the Hyperboreans and left behind them costly votive offerings bearing inscriptions in Greek letters. And in the same way, Abaris, a Hyperborean, came to Greece in ancient times and renewed the goodwill and friendship of his people towards the Delians. (38)

This semi-legendary record is considered to be of very little importance by many historians. But to other historians, very important historical facts can be embedded within a legend. And the above account is significant for several reasons. Firstly, it refers to the 19-year (i.e., 18.6 yrs) lunar node cycle, which as we have seen, is a major focus of the alignments in the design of Stonehenge. The idea of the god Apollo visiting in this cycle is a key point, which perhaps is the result over some centuries, of a compressing together in the oral traditions of the early Greeks of several different aspects to this temple.

The lunar nodal cycle is a key feature of Stonehenge, but Apollo as a sun god, is not associated with the moon. However Stonehenge itself is very much a temple designed for a cult of the sun-spirit; hence it could be thought of as a temple of Apollo. And of course Stonehenge is a circular temple, which also has a 19-year cycle built into its design. And near to Stonehenge was the sacred festival temple of Durrington Walls; this town is considered to be perhaps the largest town in Neolithic Europe.

Moreover, as we have noted earlier, the report by Diodorus Siculus refers to the Athenians and the Delians; this latter means the people of the isle of Delos. Athens was the primary cultural centre of Greece where the initiatory rituals, called the Mysteries, were very influential. But Delos is a really exceptional island in the religious life of the ancient Greeks. For the entire island is a sacred site, it is covered in the ruins of ancient temples. The island of Delos is never more than two kilometres wide, and has not only these temples, but also the ruins of many monuments, so the visitor is confronted with relics at almost every step. (40) Most of the inhabitants of Delos were priests and acolytes in the Mysteries of Apollo or other deities. Delos was regarded as the birthplace of both Apollo (the sun god) and Artemis.

It has several temples dedicated to Apollo the sun god, and two temples for Artemis. An ancient shrine to Hercules is also there, and in the remains of one temple to Apollo, there is a long hall adorned with double bull-headed columns, called the Sanctuary of the Bulls. So it was probably a monument sacred to the sun shining down from within the cosmic bull, the constellation of Taurus. Consequently, a great temple in Britain dedicated to monitoring the sun's cycle during the year (and also eclipses) would be of great interest to the priests of Delos.

Furthermore, there are the two tombs on this island known as the Tombs of the Hyperborean Maidens. These are memorials to two Hyperborean maidens who escorted votive offerings to Delos, from far away Hyperborea. This may well refer to people from Stonehenge as Cummins notes, who quotes a fascinating passage from another ancient historian Herodotus, writing about 1,000 years after these visitors in the Mycenaean era left their sacred gifts at Stonehenge. Herodotus states that there was a kind of primitive courier service between Delos and "the Hyperboreans" (that is, the British). Herodotus records that sacred gifts were taken by courier from these Hyperboreans over to the Mystery Centres on Delos. To see more about Delos, check out this site, http://www.ancient-wisdom.co.uk/greecedelos.htm

Herodotus' statements are often considered too vague to be given historical weight, especially because for many mainstream historians the identity of these Hyperborean people remains unclear. But the references to the festival city and to a circular temple and its 19 year cycle do indicate that by "the Hyperboreans" Herodotus meant Britain and hence Stonehenge, i.e., the court and priesthood responsible for this site. Like Diodorus Siculus, Herodotus also tells of an interaction between the two civilisations and of journeys made by some Hyperborean women to Delos,

> Certain sacred offerings, wrapped up in wheaten straw, come from the Hyperboreans into Scythia, whence they are taken over by the neighbouring peoples in succession until they get as far west as the Adriatic. The first Greeks to receive them are the Dodonaeans…...the Carystians take them to Tenos, and the Tenians to Delos. This is how these things are said to reach Delos at the present time {ca. 450 BC}. But on the first occasion, they were sent in the charge of two girls…to protect the girls, the Hyperboreans sent along five men with them… " (41)

Although later sources speak of the votive offering as only a simple image, it may well be that when Stonehenge was in active use by Megalithic people, the votive offerings were of a more valuable kind.

Let's return now to the discovery of ancient Grecian artefacts (actually Mycenaean or Late Minoan) found in burial mounds around Stonehenge. These were found in the 1930's, and identified by archaeologists as deriving from far away Mycenae or Knossos, and not from the local Wessex people, nor from elsewhere in Britain. (39) We noted earlier the amazing dagger with its 140,000 gold rivets; this was found in 1808, in a burial mound of an important man, presumed to be a king.

If you google "ancient jewels found in uni desk" you will come to a BBC news page from 2008 which has a colour photo of part of the gold-rivet handle.) These many gold threads symbolize the sun's rays; and their presence in the priest's or ruler's hands confirms his authority comes from the sun god. The dagger is a miracle of craftsmanship; it shows the high status of the ruler or high priest responsible for Stonehenge III, the greatest Megalithic solar (& lunar) monitoring site ever made, see illustration 9.

Other artefacts from Knossos or Mycenae that have been found in graves near Stonehenge include golden cups, gold-mounted amber discs, and also some beads of the segmented faience kind; It is significant that these beads are not found anywhere else in Western Europe. They were known in ancient eastern cultures, and they are a feature of the civilisation of Knossos in Crete, especially around 1600BC, and in ancient Egypt, few centuries later. And in addition, bone mounts of a mace have been found which are almost identical to those found at Mycenae.

Archaeologists often conclude that these Mycenaean objects were simply imported into Britain from Crete, and not brought in by their owners. However, this argument ignores the fact that there is another explanation, which is more likely. Namely, that these objects are rare ritual items, and as such would not become items of commerce. Rather, priests from other sacred sites such as Delos, Knossos and Mycenae, who were very interested in Stonehenge, brought these things with them. It was normal in antiquity for acolytes and priests to travel to other Mystery Centres. But it is also the case that some of these artefacts were apparently produced in Britain. If this theory is correct, then the implication is still remarkable; namely that Wessex craftspeople produced copies of sacred Mycenaean items. This still indicates that an interaction occurred between the priesthoods of the Aegean and of Stonehenge.

So, returning to the theory that people from Aegean sacred sites visited Stonehenge, we note that one of these graves was that of a very important woman, which contained various artefacts including a gold-bound amber disc, and a gold handled pendant in the shape of a ceremonial axe (a halberd). These indicate that she had a high secular or religious status in the community. The gold-bound amber disc, and the golden handle of the bronze dagger, is actually Minoan; and as W. A. Cummins points out, gold-bound amber discs of this kind are otherwise found only in the Cretan "Tomb of the Double Axes". But the double axe was a symbol of deity in several ancient cultures. So the object either came from a sacred ancient Cretan religious centre, or it is a replica of such a ritual object.

The fact that gold-mounted amber discs from Mycenae were buried at Stonehenge is significant. Amber is the solidified sap or life essence of the plant, and the ancients, with their holistic attitude, felt that the sun's forces were symbiotically linked to the life of a plant. It is then no surprise that amber is viewed in ancient lore as a substance that was somehow linked to the sun. And gold was also seen as an expression of solar energies. So these discs are an expression of the worship of a sun deity; a worship shared by both the Minoan priesthood and the Wessex priests.

So, there are two possibilities for these special artefacts being left in the Salisbury plains. Either that people from the higher ranks of priesthood in pre-classical Grecian sacred sites visited Stonehenge and brought these artefacts. Or these visitors showed the designs to the Wessex priesthood, whose artisans then decided to made the sacred objects locally.

9   Remarkable dagger of the sun god religion

From a grave near
Stonehenge. In its
design this is a
Mycenaean dagger,
but it may have been
made in Wiltshire.

With bronze blade
and wooden handle,
it has gold bands,
made up of many
tiny golden rivets.

In fact there are
140,000 golden
rivets !

A miracle of
craftsmanship,
it gave authority to
the sun god's agent:
the ruler or high
high priest at
Stonehenge

(Computer graphic
based on sketches
and photos of clust-
ers of its gold rivets)

88

In any event, it appears likely that the religious interaction with cosmic cycles undertaken at Stonehenge was not carried out in isolation, but shared with people from islands and cities around the Mediterranean region. We can now briefly look at some other Megalithic sites to deepen our understanding of the Wessex people who built Stonehenge.

Similar Megalithic monuments in Ireland

The most famous and sophisticated of all monuments from the Megalithic people in Ireland is the famous Newgrange site. There are about 150 stone circles in Ireland. Jack Roberts lists 100 of these in the region of Derry and Cork, and identifies an astronomical orientation for many of these.[15] In the site near the Boyne River, where Newgrange is located, there are many burial mounds and other sacred monuments.

Newgrange consists of a stone chamber covered with soil, having inside a long corridor and, off to the sides, various chambers. It is located at Newgrange, 30 miles north of Dublin, on a low ridge, overlooking a bend in the Boyne River. It is a mound some 269 ft (82m) in diameter, and 30 ft (9.1m) high. Its south side faces the river and has been given a band of bright white quartz.

In the middle of this wall of quartz rock is the entrance, in front of which is a large stone, that has been carved with intricate, typically Celtic scrollwork. Inside this mound is a passageway some 62 ft long (19 m) and tall enough for a person to walk along without having to bend down. At the end of the passageway is a chamber, made from huge stones, which is cross-shaped and about 20 ft (6 m) high. At each end of the cross is a burial place, a hollowed stone, and indeed these did at some time contain skeletons.

This monument is in fact classified as a passage-tomb, but the interesting point is that it has features which clearly indicate a connection with religious activity. That is to say, although it

---

[15] See his *The Stone Circles of Cork & Derry: an astronomical Guide*, Bandia Publishing

indisputably became a burial site, the high probability exists that, in the first phase of its existence, it was a religious site, which was later used as a tomb. As we saw earlier this happened at Stonehenge. The intermingling of temples for the after-life and initiatory sites is not uncommon at a sacred site. In Egypt there was a funerary temple built right outside the Great Pyramid, and other sites in Egypt may have been originally built for religious purpose, and then later became used as a tomb. The mysteries of the after-life and of the religious-initiatory process are symbiotically linked.

Archaeological work at Newgrange has shown that the roof of the monument was very carefully constructed; it is corbelled, i.e., has overhanging slabs placed up on top of each other. This is the same type of corridor that we find in the Great Pyramid in Egypt, in its Grand Gallery. And we conclude that the corbelled effect was intended to give the acolyte the feeling of the various heavenly realms that their priests believed exist in ever higher splendour above the earthly realm. During the construction of Newgrange, drainage channels were made for the rain; the seams of these channels were sealed with a putty-like substance, made from burned soil. This roof was then covered over with a huge amount of material, layers of water-smoothed pebbles and turf, forming the mound.

But, furthermore, the entire interior construction was also astronomically oriented, and although the entrance was sealed off from the light, above the entrance a narrow slot was created. The archaeologists who first discovered this in 1969, Michael and Claire O'Kelly, had a hunch as to the purpose of this unusual slot, and positioned themselves at the end of the passageway on the morning of the winter solstice (Dec. 21st). They noted that four minutes after sunrise the light began to enter the chamber, eventually flooding it with light, fading away after 17 minutes. This happens in fact about one week before the solstice, and lasts until about one week after.

So, the question arises, is this monument a passage tomb that revealed the midwinter sun for the dead? Or is it an initiatory passage chamber, where the living observed the beginning of the 12 holy nights of Yuletide (as this festival was later called)? We have seen that, on the one hand, there is a tomb with an alignment to the Moon for the deceased, at Kintraw, but these are very rare.

But on the other hand, we have seen that in the Orkney Islands there are cairns with passage chambers that are designed for initiatory purpose. Indeed there are more such cairns with passage chambers made by the Megalithic people. In the vicinity of Newgrange in Ireland are at least three such sites, which appear to be either passage burial chambers, or initiatory chambers; these are at Dowth, and at Knowth.

Knowth is one of the largest and most sophisticated of the 300 or so cairns with passageways inside it in Ireland, and in fact, it and Newgrange and Dowth are all situated in the Boyne Valley, where there are many tombs which are obviously gravesites in this area. Naturally, such monuments are normally classified as passage-tombs. So, we have here a situation like that at the Giza plateau, where many gravesites are placed around a prominent initiatory monument, i.e., the Great Pyramid, and at Stonehenge where sacred temples are sited in a burial area.

A monument that was originally an initiatory place became used as a burial site. At Knowth, the large mound is surrounded by 17 smaller ones. The oval-shaped main mound varies in diameter from 262-311 ft (80-95m), with a height between 40-50ft (12 - 15m). However what makes Knowth so impressive, and raises the possibility that it was not designed as a tomb, is the artwork that it contains.

Inside, the walls are extensively decorated with Celtic spirals and around the outside, on the so-called kerb stones, there are quite specific diagrams of the sun and other stars, These astronomical or cosmic symbols can be a decoration for a tomb, but here it seems that the purpose of the site was not that of burial, but of some initiatory process, because this place is oriented to the midwinter sunrise, and also it has other astronomical illustrations on stones set around the perimeter of the mound. The situation is similar at another site nearby, at Dowth, where again an earth-covered cairn contains extensive passages as well as ornate decorations.

Furthermore, the orientation of the chamber at Dowth has some similarity to the Celtic sites we noted earlier, although it does not have the extreme precision of the Externsteine. Sunlight penetrates the chamber in the winter months, and illuminates the very back of the chamber around the winter solstice. This has been researched by Anne-Marie Moroney, see her website, http://www.knowth.com/dowth-sunsets. These Irish monuments show us how the mind-set of the Megalithic people, and thus the builders of Stonehenge, was deeply attracted to monitoring and experiencing celestial events. Their sacred sites were skilfully aligned to celestial events.

Now let's see the nature of mainstream archaeological views on the alignments of Stonehenge, and the limitations of these.

Chapter Eight

Archaeological views about Stonehenge

Lionel Sims from the University of East London in his thesis, "The solarization of the Moon" takes the views of John North to task pointing out his errors, but arguing that Stonehenge is indeed nevertheless based on a SW orientation as North insists, but for a different reason to that of North. (35) However, like North, Sims is not convinced about the NE summer solstice sunrise orientation of Stonehenge, nor the other aspects it obviously has: the eclipse monitoring, the key seasonal sunrise or setting observation, the lunar major standstills. Nor, of course, are the shadow-fields factored in.

Indeed the fact that with Stonehenge the summer solstice sunrise is in almost direct alignment to the winter sunset (and has various right-angled alignments, because it is sited at 51 degrees north) is called "an unintended and fortuitous consequence of the monument's geographical position". We shall look at some of his arguments because they summarize excellently the prevailing erroneous academic attitudes to Stonehenge, and confirm the errors of North.

Argument by Sims:

> Over the last three decades, one finding is that the stone monuments of the late Neolithic and Early Bronze Age in the British Isles have an orientation towards the southwest which pairs alignments on the setting winter sun and the moon at its southern major or minor standstill moonset limits (Ruggles/Burl)

My Response:

This is very likely true; but Stonehenge has a different orientation. The southerly moonset at the major standstill is not visible (and the minor ones are mainly excluded, too). Stonehenge has its major orientation to the summer solstice sunrise in the NE, but in addition its trilithons are actually oriented to the remarkable lunar nodes standstill phenomena, and to the moonrise in summer, and in winter and the moonset in winter. It is also oriented to the winter solstice sunset, and winter sunrise. See illustration 10 for a diagram illustrating the theory of a winter NW orientation of Stonehenge.

Sims:

> It is unclear where the centre of Stonehenge lies. It is not marked by any stone (Clealet al. 1995; Ruggles 1999a), nor is the Avenue aligned on the centre of the sarsen circle (Atkinson 1979, 94-5). The absence of a precise viewing position is important, since even changing from one eye to the other alters the alignment by many solar diameters. In the absence of any criterion by which a central viewing position can be fixed, no definite alignment can be claimed.

Response:

Actually, the trilithons are designed to allow a person to know when special astronomical events are approaching, culminating and receding; the precise minute of actual occurrence was not so important. They did not want, like modern people, to just know the mathematically precise minute, out of abstract interest, and then get back to their everyday life.[16] The Druidic observer has been monitoring the approach of an eclipse or a solstice, a standstill, etc, for some days and now they simply have to place themselves in that spot from which, previous experience has taught them this can be seen, at its actual occurrence. This is where the narrow line-of-sight opens up between the sarsens. Various astronomers have verified that this observation point is near the centre of the great sarsen circle.

Sims:

> When the now prostrate Slaughter Stone is stood upright from its present position, it entirely obscures the view of the Heel Stone from the centre of

---

[16] Nothing illustrates this modern approach more than the New Year's Day celebrations; the New Year used to always begin on the Spring Equinox, until a mentally ill French monarch in the 1564 insisted on this date being set in the winter.

Stonehenge, blocking any view of a Heel Stone alignment on the summer sunrise.

Response:
The Slaughter Stone now lies flat by the Avenue entrance and it was associated in the late 18th century in a fanciful way with rituals of sacrifices, connected with Druidism. As Hawkins points out, although Inigo Jones and John Aubrey sketched it as upright where it now lies, a lot of romantic reconstruction has been put into their sketches. Initially, it may indeed have been upright, but in a different position, perhaps as one of the two gateway stones which at one time existed between the Helan Stone and the sarsens. In this original position, it would not have blocked the line-of-sight.

Sims:

> Within the darkening mass of stone at winter solstice sunset, a Heel Stone observer would have seen a burst of light, as the sun seemed to set into the Altar stone at the apparent centre of the monument.

Response:
This theoretical reconstruction may well be true; it shows only that the commencement of the Yuletide season was important. Hence the SW aspect of the monument was carefully worked out to allow this. But all five trilithons are designed to provide key celestial alignments; the major alignment for shadow-fields observing, via the Helan Stone was always to the NE, for the midsummer sunrise. The SW alignment is but one of several.

Sims

> Stonehenge has, as its primary orientation, a South-West orientation, because the lower window {formed in the SW by the Grand Trilithon} is aligned on the winter solstice sunset. Second, looking from the left side of the Heel Stone, an upper window is framed again within the grand trilithon uprights, but now between the upper surface of the closest lintel of the

outer sarsen circle and the lower surface of the protruding grand trilithon lintel. This upper window, directly above the lower window, is aligned on the southern minor standstill setting moon. The first alignment occurs once every year, but the second occurs only once in 19 years. {So there is a double alignment happening in the SW}

Response:
The above description of Sims seems complex, but it is not, just see illustration 10 for a clear diagram illustrating the theory. The diagram illustrating the viewpoint of North, in illustration 11, shows this supposed second window, by which he means a small gap between two horizontal slabs. But note that this is to be seen from the shadow-making Cover Stone, which is a distance of some 128 yards (117 metres) away! So in truth, nothing would be seen, it's just too far away. Sims now shows that North was quite incorrect! Sims quotes from John North...

> "The grand trilithon was so designed as to allow for two key observations from the Heel Stone, one of the setting midwinter sun at its base, the other of the setting moon at minor southern standstill at its top... As the moon set, its last glint within the window would have gradually shifted, day by day, from the right-hand end to the left, and it would then have reversed. ...{If a normal Moon motion was} normal then a minor standstill {by contrast} has a touch of the miraculous about it, and perhaps this was the reason for paying so much attention to it."

And now Sims counters this, by saying that North (1996) seems to suggest that standstills are the lunar equivalent of the sun's solstices, because at the southern minor standstill, seen in the grand trilithon upper window at Stonehenge, according to John North, the setting moon "would have gradually shifted, day by day, from the right-hand end to the left, and it would then have reversed" (North 1996, 474-5). Sims then points out that the lunar still-stand is **not** a lingering, striking phenomenon; it would not have been a strikingly long-term display to the observer inside the circle, looking to the SW. For as Sims says,

> The moon sets at its south-western horizon limit only once every 27 nights, and does not stay at this position for a week, as do the winter solstice sunsets. The very next night, moonsets begin to move to their north-western horizon limit, arriving there 13 or 14 nights later, to then immediately start moving southwards. Therefore, unlike the sun, the south-western limit to the moon's horizon setting point is not characterized by a week in which the moonsets appear stationary.

In other words, there **were no significant, awe-inspiring, lunar motions at this supposed upper window,** involving the moon appearing at its minor standstill, in a remarkable way, on the winter solstice evening, so North's core argument for a SW orientation **is entirely wrong**! This is a valuable and competent observation of Sims, undermining North's conclusions as to the very purpose of Stonehenge.

However, this is only the first major error of John North, for Sims then shows the other very major error in North's core argument for aligning Stonehenge to the SW, (as we know it is to the NE and the summer sunrise). Namely that a moon at the winter solstice, on the time of the southern standstills, (minor or major) **always presents a dark moon**, i.e., **one that cannot be seen**, as it is a New Moon (!). Sims then says, correctly:

> The upper window of the grand trilithon is aligned on the southern, not northern, standstill and this trilithon generates a full moon at the summer solstice, not {at the} winter solstice, this generates a dark moon, a New Moon (and therefore no full Moon will appear then!).

For Stonehenge to do what North erroneously argues that it does, it would have to be aligned to the north-western lunar standstills, not the south-westerly ones! So Professor North's core argument is shown to be false. Sims then proceeds to argue that the two outer stone circles are a kind of indirect complex helix-form, presenting in a coded way, key lunar and solar motions. We need not follow his argument here (readers can download it). He then points out that, as we have just noted, the Moon at the southern standstill is indeed aligned to the winter solstice sunset, and it could theoretically appear, above the setting sun, just as North also argues; (except North thought it was visible, but, Sims points out again, the moon is then invisible).

But, remarkably, Sims still goes on from here to argue that this idea, of a SW orientation is still a really key element of Stonehenge! This non-visible New Moon at the lunar standstill is proof, he says, that Stonehenge has a SW orientation, but for a different reason to that given (erroneously) by North.

Sims' crucial point is this; that Stonehenge is intended to bracket together the (invisible) southern minor standstill Moon with the winter solstice setting sun, whose last rays would appear just underneath the top of the Grand Trilithon. Now what is he saying here? Before we proceed, we need to bear in mind two very significant things. A lunar standstill occurs only once in 19 years; and we also need to note that of course, the night of the winter solstice sunset is the darkest, longest night of the year, because the Sun is at its farthest from the hemisphere. Let's hear what Sims thinks is the reason for a SW orientation of the immensely complex Stonehenge project undertaken by the Megalithic people,

> "Therefore, at Stonehenge {looking to the SW} the winter solstice sunset is bracketed with the southern minor standstill moonset, and this will ensure that, once every 19 years, the winter solstice sunset is

associated with the dark {invisible} moon at the start of the longest and darkest night of the year."

He goes to argue that this means that they have created a wonderful symbolic statement; "by bracketing this dark {invisible} moon with the setting winter sun, each mimics the other in their properties of signalling the onset of darkness."

Response:
Well, what do we make of this? We need to consider several really striking facts here, when assessing this struggle of non-holistic views to explain the core purpose of the holistic Wessex Druids who built Stonehenge. Firstly, as we noted above, the alignment only occurs every 18.6 years. So firstly, in between these 18.6 years cycles, **Stonehenge has very little use** (!!). Secondly, it is supposedly to be seen when standing at the Heel Stone (Cover Stone). For remember, to the archaeologist the entire complex, its vast and indeed uniquely great megalithic engineering is almost pointless, so you don't bother entering the circle. So, the truly vast effort of creating **the stone circles becomes almost irrelevant** (!).

Thirdly, is it said that the moon "was to be seen"? Well again, look at the diagram (illustration 11) and see how the tiny gap below the Grand Trilithon and the top of the sarsens in front of it, has enough space for only a tiny part of the moon; and remember as we just note, you are gazing at this tiny sight from across the diameter of the circle and also over the Cover-Stone, which is about 128 yards (117m) away. **You would see almost nothing.**

But all of these points become insignificant when one also recollects that exactly as Sims points out, this southern minor standstill Moon **is invisible**, it is in a New Moon phase! There is nothing to see, **nothing at all! There would be a kind of grand No-Show.**

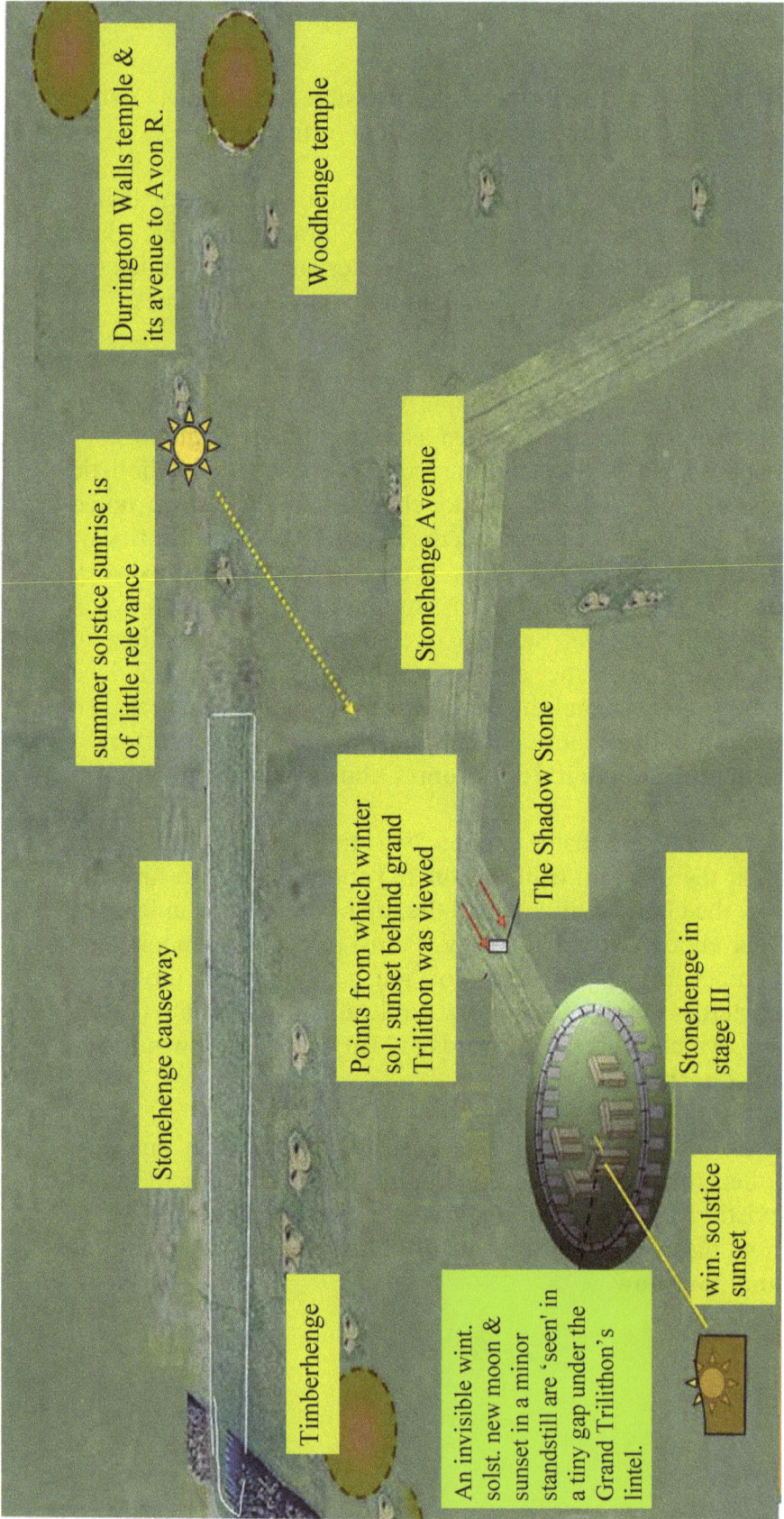

Durrington Walls temple & its avenue to Avon R.

Woodhenge temple

summer solstice sunrise is of little relevance

Stonehenge Avenue

Stonehenge causeway

Points from which winter sol. sunset behind grand Trilithon was viewed

The Shadow Stone

Timberhenge

Stonehenge in stage III

An invisible wint. solst. new moon & sunset in a minor standstill are 'seen' in a tiny gap under the Grand Trilithon's lintel.

win. solstice sunset

10 Winter Orientation theory. Most of the stones and trilithons are irrelevant, as are the celestial alignments. Instead, the invisible new moon and winter solstice sunset are 'viewed' through a tiny gap above the Grand Trilithon, from over by the Shadow Stone.

The basis for a SW orientation: the tiny gap below the Grand Trilithon's lintel: seen from the Shadow Stone, 117 m away. When viewed from the actual distance, the gap becomes truly too tiny to 'observe' the new (invisible) moon.

The gap for observing North's invisible moon, or to 'bracket' Sims invisible moon with the midwinter setting sun

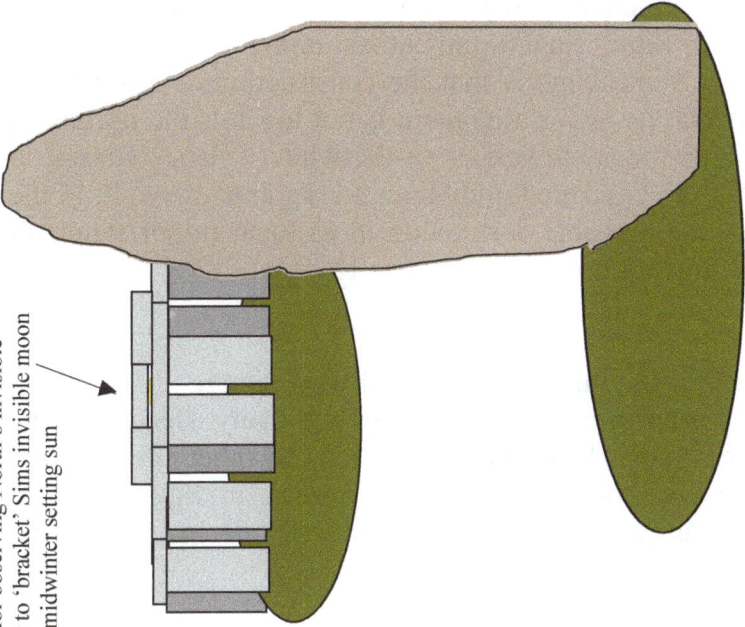

11 **The SW orientation argument:** at Stonehenge has its primary orientation to the SW. The dark moon at a minor standstill is to be 'not-seen' in the tiny gap between the Grand Trilithons capstone, & the top of the other sarsens in front of it. This is even tinier from 128 yards (117 m) away.

So, according to Sims' argument, Stonehenge has an alignment created at a vast cost to the Neolithic society of Britain which, once every 19 years, offered a No-Show. And North's argument was false in two ways, for the moon does not make any dramatic motions (in a minor standstill), and is anyway invisible in a standstill on the evening of Dec 21st. But Sims' argument is even less valid. Namely, yes, the moon is invisible at this time, but nevertheless, every 19 years that's what you looked out for! **An invisible moon coupled with the small section of the weak rays from the setting winter sun, seen in the tiny slot of the Grand Trilithon**.

Even in a modern well-educated society, with some capacity for subtle symbolism, this would be asking a lot. But to expect a site that offered a No-Show once every 19 years, to become a revered sacred site for the unschooled Megalithic people seems truly unlikely. The Megalithic builders spent perhaps 1.5 million man-hours building this stone circle and called upon a remarkable holistic (psychic) intelligence to ascertain the precise celestial coordinates; but 90% of this is of little or no value! Just the Grand Trilithon and the stone in front of it have any use.

Obviously this viewpoint is also wrong. Stonehenge was created for much more than the very minor events that Sims is postulating. Sims' final argument, summing up archaeology's attitude to Stonehenge is that the construction of Stonehenge suggests that its major alignment is not towards the northeast, but towards the southwest, onto the winter solstice sunset, in order that the bracketed midwinter sunset and, above it, in the tiny gap, the invisible dark moon in its lunar minor standstill can be seen {not-seen!} once every 19 years.

Conclusion: the many purposes of Stonehenge
We have seen in our exploration of the many aspects of this great site, that it had similar functions to other great sacred sites, such as those on the Giza plateau in Egypt, and in Ireland. Namely, it was a place primarily designed to assist

people in their interaction with spiritual energies associated with the sun, the stars and the moon. Hence at Stonehenge, and the nearby Durrington Walls, just as on the Giza plateau of Egypt, processions and rituals took place in a temple and also along a grand causeway at solstice or equinox times, or before an eclipse, or at a lunar standstill. On the Salisbury Plains this occurred on one of the Avenues that went down towards the Avon; and at Giza, it was on one of the Causeways that led down to the Nile River. Processions took place as part of festivities honouring the gods or bringing initiation to an acolyte. And occasionally there were also no doubt some funeral rites.

This is why Stonehenge has not only a grand Avenue, but also has the immensely demanding features of accurately aligned stone circles and trilithons, allowing observation of the heavens at the solstice and equinox, or when lunar standstills were occurring. And through the use of huge stone uprights, observation of the interaction between terrestrial and celestial energies could be made from within the large shadow-fields these stones created.

Some significant Megalithic sites with similar features to those of Stonehenge and Maes Howe are also found in nearby Ireland. But so important and sophisticated was Stonehenge, that priests and people seeking healing or spiritual experiences, came to Britain from ancient pre-Grecian Mysteries to visit this greatest of all Megalithic sites. Throughout this book we have endeavoured to show that the entire purpose and design of Stonehenge was to allow a focus on several lines-of-sight, to enable precise knowledge of complex lunar node motions and solar key days. But secondly, the focus of Stonehenge was also to allow shadow-fields to be created, at key solar times. And amidst the bluestones circles, healing rituals were no doubt also enacted.

And whilst Stonehenge also served as a place for a limited number of burials, this was only a secondary use. (The theory that the stones are basically ancestral stones, bringing memory of deceased ancestors is very shallow, ignoring as it does the entire sophisticated astronomical alignments and shadow-fields.) So, we close this book about the Megalithic people and their greatest sacred site, having revealed we hope, some more of Stonehenge's wonderful significance. The building of sacred sites by the Megalithic people ceased about 1,000 BC. But the Celtic cultures which arose at that time, as the successors to the similar Megalithic people, continued in a general way the reverence of nature and interest in monitoring key astronomical events.

This Celtic spirituality, reflecting the old spirituality of the Megalithic people, continued on until the Hellenistic Age, or even into the Middle Ages, depending on which part of Europe is in focus. But in the modern era, the astonishing celestial alignments and shadow-fields of Stonehenge, as well as its high reputation amongst people in Mystery Centres elsewhere in Europe, had faded from memory. The ruins of its complex stone circles and trilithons, remained an unsolvable riddle, until Gerard Hawkins astronomical research began to unlock its mysteries.

APPENDIX The Saros Cycle and blocking of Carbon 14

In the early years of modern astronomy, scientists thought that space was literally empty, but by the middle of last century it was becoming apparent that this dismal, skeletal view of the cosmos was extremely short-sighted. The universe began to be seen as far more sophisticated and subtle and multi-layered. The change came from both theoretical mathematical investigations into the forces at work in keeping the structure of the galaxy intact, and from increasingly refined capacity to detect ever more subtle electro-magnetic energies.

Various energies, called cosmic rays, were discovered raying into the earth's atmosphere; and here they are striking subtle electro-magnetic energy-particles. Prominent amongst these minute particles is what is called an isotope (an incomplete, non-physical, energized form of matter). In particular these impacted upon the common substance carbon, in an isotopic form, known as C14. The very concept of an energy-particle is intriguing, for it really means that science has had to make room for an holistic view of creation, in which substance (in this case, carbon), exists in a form which is not yet material, not yet condensed into a material or tangible state.

The sun is known to be pouring these subtle energies out into the solar system in huge quantities and with great force, and this is called the solar wind. In the solar wind are many important trace elements and metals etc, which form the building blocks of matter on our planet. The biggest production in the atmosphere of these cosmogenic radionuclides occurs when cosmic rays coming from either the sun or from elsewhere in the galaxy, interact with atmospheric gases, see illustration 12. These particles are known as "cosmogenic radionuclides", meaning that they have been brought into being by cosmic energies impacting on the Earth's upper atmosphere.

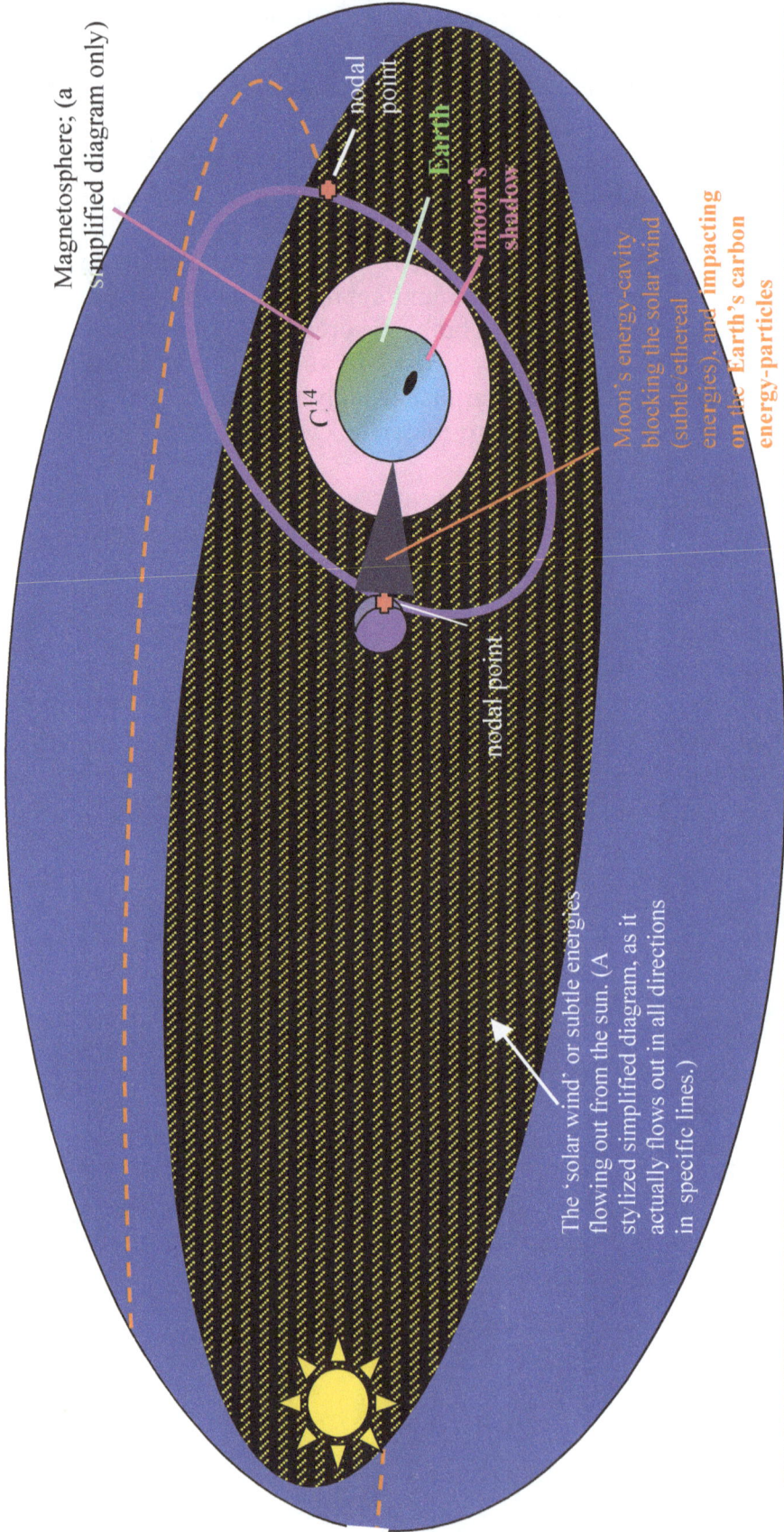

12 The Saros & a solar eclipse, and the **Earth's magnetosphere** during a sun-moon-earth alignment. The sun's light is blocked by the moon, creating a shadow on the Earth, but in a Saros cycle, as the moon aligns to a node, it also blocks subtle cosmic energies (solar wind, etc). A simplified diagram, not to scale.

Graphics: © author

Magnetosphere; (a simplified diagram only)

nodal point

Earth

moon's shadow

C^{14}

Moon's energy-cavity blocking the solar wind (subtle ethereal energies), and impacting on the Earth's carbon energy-particles

nodal point

The 'solar wind' or subtle energies flowing out from the sun. (A stylized simplified diagram, as it actually flows out in all directions in specific lines.)

Concentrations of cosmogenic radionuclides vary in the atmosphere with time and location; variations are day-to-day, seasonal, longitudinal, and are also sunspot-cycle related. Awareness of this process occurred many decades ago, and has brought about a radical enlivening of astronomical views of creation, adding a whole new dimension of subtle energies to what was a repellent, static and lifeless empty universe. From our study of the 56 Aubrey holes, and the 19 bluestone inner circle (or horse-shoe), we know that this Saros cycle, as the cosmic configuration that causes eclipses, was of major interest to the Megalithic people.

Now from upper atmosphere research astronomers are aware of a change occurring in a prominent energy-particle (so-called cosmogenic radionuclide) existing in the atmosphere, namely, Carbon 14 (or C14). Every 18 years there is a brief change in the inherent strength of this energy-particle, in its especial frequency, as it pulses through the atmosphere. [17] Two scientists, Sonett and Smith, have investigated this prominent celestial cycle that produces a variation in these subtle energy-particles, with its impact on the atmosphere, occurring about every 18 years. This is the same number of years as the Saros cycle, the cycle that can cause an eclipse, if the sun, moon and Earth are in the correct positions.

The effect of this variation can be detected in the rings of trees, which, as they grow, absorb these tiny particles. The C14 content in a tree ring corresponds to that of radio-carbon in atmospheric carbonic acid during the growth of the ring. Sonett and Smith write that they "…used the C14 records in Pacific Northwest pine tree ring cellulose as the basic data from which the key result of their research was drawn".

They put the question as to whether such a change of C14 (occurring in a rhythm of 18 yrs) can be due to something happening at the top of the atmosphere. They focus on a fascinating feature in the subtle energy fields associated with

---

[17] That is, scientifically, there is a change in its 'power spectral density'.

the moon, pointing out that on the side of the moon which is turned away from the sun, there exists a kind of energy-cavity, very similar to a shadow being made by any object, as it blocks the sunlight, see illustration 12.

This cavity has a reduced presence of those subtle energies sent out from the sun, called the solar wind. Now it is already known that every 11 years there is a change in the C14 presence in the atmosphere, and it has been concluded that this is due to the effect of sunspots, which are at maximum every 11 years. But there is also a change every 18 years. Now we know that every 18 years the moon, in its orbit around our planet, comes to the node point, the place where the pathway of the moon and that of the sun intersect each other. We know that this will cause an eclipse, if the sun and moon and earth are all aligned.

But as the scientists point out, this blocking of solar energies by the moon happens every 18 years, regardless of whether there is an eclipse or not. At such a time, in this cycle as the lunar node cycle is completed, this cavity is even less influenced by solar energies. This lunar energy-cavity (or plasma cavity), acts like a shadow extending out a long way from the dark side of the moon, and blocks these subtle solar energies. This temporarily darkened lunar cone-shaped area reaches Earthwards, and affects the Earth's own magnetic field, or magnetosphere. Sonett and Smith report that the Earth's magnetosphere is exposed to the Moon's hydro-magnetic shadow for about 1 hour every 18 years, see illustration 12. It is this moving of a darkened lunar energy field, through our planet's atmosphere that causes this reduction in the carbon content.

References:
Cosmic ray anomaly: the Saros cycle and a lunar perturbation, by Charles P. Sonett (Department of Planetary Sciences, Lunar and Planetary Laboratory University of Arizona Tucson) and Leonard A. Smith (Mathematical Institute

University of Oxford, Oxford, U.K.) Geophysical Research Letters, Vol. 26, No. 11, pps. 1569-1572, June 1, 1999

REFERENCES

1 See for example, John Mathews, Taliesin: Shamanism and Bardic mysteries in Britain and Ireland, The Aquarian Press, London, 1991

2 Mathews, Taliesin, p 162

3 The Cambridge guide to literature in English, Ian Ousby & Doris Lessing, Camb Univ Press, 1993 p 36.

4 Elucidated by E. Merry The Flaming Door, J. Mathews, in *Taliesin*, and L. Spence, in his The Mysteries of Britain & his The History and Origins of Druidism

5 http://www.monumental.uk.com/site/research/proj/acoustics/dwarfie.html

6 http://www.orkneyjar.com/history/maeshowe/index.html

7 http://www.orkneyjar.com/history/maeshowe/solstice.htm)

8 http://www.archtext.co.uk/onlinetexts/britains_past/chapter07

9 Evan Hadingham, Early Man and the Cosmos, Heinemann, London, 1983

10 Wood, John Edwin. Sun, Moon and Standing Stones. Oxford: Oxford University Press, 1978, quoted by Helen Benigni http://www.themystica.com/mystica/articles/ the_doors_of_precession_lunar_deities.html)

11 Evan Hadingham, Secrets of Stonehenge, in The World's Last Mysteries, Reader's Digest, 1987, p. 85.

12 Stonehenge Riverside Project: New Approaches to Durrington Walls Mike Parker Pearson : /www.shef.ac.uk/archaeology/research/stonehenge

13 Richard Mudhar www.megalithia.com/Stonehenge. Richard Mudhar offers a fascinating and detailed view of the construction of Stonehenge in its various phases

14 A wide variety of books and websites provide these statistical facts, incl. R. Castleden, The Making of Stonehenge, and M. Balfour, Stonehenge and its Mysteries.

15 news.bbc.co.uk/2/hi/science/nature/ "Stonehenge builders' houses found".

16 The Legend of Stonehenge, www. math.nus.edu.sg/aslaksen/gem-projects/html/Stonehenge)

17 http://www.christiaan.com/stonehenge/index.

18 See www.experiencefestival.com/a/Stonehenge_-
_Development_of _ Stonehenge/id/

19 Rodney Castleden, The Making of Stonehenge p.134

20 Gerald Hawkins, Stonehenge Decoded, p 47 Souvenir
press, London,1965

21http://www.math.nus.edu.sg/aslaksen/gen-
projects/hn/Stonehenge

22 http://www.wwu.edu/depts/skywise/stonehenge_align.html

23http://www.math.nus.edu.sg/aslaksen/gen-
projects/hn/Stonehenge

24 http://www.wwu.edu/depts/skywise/stonehenge_align.html

25 www.bbc.co.uk/history…. John Farren, BBC Timewatch
editor

26 http://www.math.nus.edu.sg/aslaksen/gem-
projects/hm/Stonehenge.pdf

27http://witcombe.sbc.edu/earthmysteries/EMStonehengeD.ht
ml

28 C.A. Newham, The astronomical significance of
Stonehenge, John Blackburn Ltd, Leeds, 1972

29http://www.space.com/scienceastronomy/astronomy/stoneh
enge_eclipse_000119. html

30 In Francis Hitchins, "Megalithic Engineering", The World
Atlas of Mysteries, Pan Books, 1978

31 James Frazer's unabridged 13 vol. work, The Golden
Bough, and Hastings Encyclopaedia of Religion and Ethics
(13 vols) record many examples of the belief in many cultures,
about malignant influences being unleashed in an eclipse.

32 F. Marian McNeill, A Calendar of Scottish national
festivals, vol 3, W. Maclellan, Glasgow 1961

33 John North, Stonehenge, Neolithic man and the Cosmos,
Harper Collins, London, 1996

34 R. MacAlister, "Stone Monuments", Hastings
Encyclopaedia of Religion and Ethics, Vol. Eleven, p 880,
Edinburgh, 1920.

35 Jacques Briard, Carnac, Land of Megaliths, Editons Jean-
Paul Gisserot, 2000

36 Lionel Sims, The Solarization of the Moon, manipulated
knowledge at Stonehenge. (A thesis from University of East
London: http://journals.Cambridge.org)

37 Helan: see A Thesaurus of Old English, J. Roberts, J A Roberts, et al, Rodopi Press, 2000; and The Oxford Dictionary of English Etymology, edit. C.T. Onions, OUP, 1966, and Glossary from Bright's Anglo-Saxon reader, at www.ling.upenn.edu/~kuristo/germanic/oe_bright_ glossary

38 Quoted in W.A. Cummins, King Arthur's place in Pre-history, A. Sutton, publ. Dover, 1992.

39 Cummins, King Arthur's Place in Pre-history.

40 E. Pepper & J. Wilcock, Magical and Mystical Sites, Abacus, London, 1978,

41 Herodotus, the Histories, trans. Aubrey de Selincourt, Penguin, Harmondsworth, 1978, p. 281-283

Picture credits

1 The author

2 The author

3 The author

4 The author

5 Above, Lanyon: Wikimedia Commons, photographer : **Olaf Tausch** 23 June 2009

The use of this image by the author does not imply in any way that the photographer supports or agrees with any viewpoint expressed in this book

5 Below, Trevethy Quoit, Wikimedia Commons; a drawing from 1842, by William Borlases's sketch of the quoit in his book, Observations on the Antiquities, Historical and Monumental of the county of Cornwall of 1754. Placed on Wikimedia by Cyrus Redding.

6 Above, Crucuno quoit; Wikimedia Commons, photographer, **Myrabella**, 23 June 2009 CC-BY-SA-3.0

The use of this image by the author does not imply in any way that the photographer supports or agrees with any viewpoint expressed in this book

6 Below, Mane-Kerioned; Wikimedia Commons, photographer, **Kamel15,** August 2008. GNU license, Attribution-Share Alike 3.0 Unported

The use of this image by the author does not imply in any way that the photographer supports or agrees with any viewpoint expressed in this book

7 The author

8 The author

9 The author

10 The author

11 Left: The author

Right: Free stock photo by **Duncan Harris** on www.veezle.com/photo/934201/Stonehenge-from-the-heel-stone; available under Creative Commons Attribution3.0 Unported. The use of this image by the author does not imply in any way that the photographer supports or agrees with any viewpoint expressed in this book

12 The author

INDEX

www.ingramcontent.com/pod-product-compliance
Lightning Source LLC
Chambersburg PA
CBHW081332090426
42737CB00017B/3103